A YEAR OF GRA[illegible] MARY
Rediscovering her Presence
and
her Role in our Consecration

VERITAS

English language edition
first published 1987 by
Veritas Publications
7-8 Lower Abbey Street
Dublin 1

Original French language edition
published 1987 by
Librairie Arthème Fayard

ISBN 0 86217 279 9

All Scripture extracts are taken from the *New Jerusalem Bible,* published and copyright 1985 by Darton, Longman & Todd Ltd., and Doubleday & Co. Inc., and are used by permission of the publishers.

Cover illustration:
Panel from Ascension window by Evie Hone, at Kingscourt Parish Church, Cavan. Reproduction courtesy of Dr Michael Wynne.

Cover design: Eddie McManus
Typesetting: Printset & Design Ltd, Dublin
Printed in the Republic of Ireland by
Mount Salus Press Ltd, Dublin

CONTENTS

TRANSLATOR'S PREFACE

Father Laurentin, *a peritus* (expert) at the Second Vatican Council, participated in the drafting of the conciliar text on the Blessed Virgin. He is a member of both International Mariological Academies in Rome and Vice-President of the French Society of Marian Studies. For over twenty years he has kept apace with everything on the subject of the Virgin Mary that appeared in scientific and pastoral journals *(Revue des Sciences Philosophiques et Théologiques* and *Vie Spirituelle).*

He continues to lecture on Mary in several universities in France, Italy and at the Marian Center of the University of Dayton, Ohio. During the last five summers, he has been received enthusiastically by the graduate students of the Pontifical Catechetical Institutes of Arlington, Virginia and the Archdiocese of New York respectively.

René Laurentin is recognised as the most internationally renowned specialist on the subject of our Lady. This book may be said to crown his scientific and pastoral work in a manner which is both profound yet simple. The catechetical dimension of his treatment of our Lady is also quite apparent.

This theologian knows how to write with the clarity of a professional journalist without neglecting to come right to the point of what is essential for restoring to our Blessed Lady, so frequently forgotten in our day, her relevance for the Church and each one of us.

May this work assist us in delving more profitably into the spiritual riches of our Holy Father's encyclical for this Marian Year, *Redemptoris Mater.*

It has been a great privilege for me to translate this beautiful work. I have done so by way of personal homage and gratitude to *Notre Dame* of Paris, under whose protection and at whose statue I was able to entrust the then aborning future of the now Pontificial Archdiocesan Catechetical Institute back in 1977.

Reverend Monsignor Michael J. Wrenn
Director
Pontifical Archdiocesan Catechetical Institute of St Joseph's Seminary
Dunwoodie, Yonkers, New York 10704
Pentecost Sunday 1987

INTRODUCTION

A YEAR WITH MARY

On 1 January 1987, during his homily at St Peter's in Rome, the Pope announced 'a year dedicated to Mary', as we look toward the year 2000 . . . an extended year which 'will open on Pentecost Sunday', 7 June 1987 and end fourteen months later, 'on the Feast of the Assumption', 15 August 1988.

Where are we going?

1 What was the reason for this sudden and unexpected decision? This is precisely what this first chapter will attempt to explain since this proposal of John Paul II is rooted in some personal and ecclesial secrets which certainly ought to be shared.

2 In order to be a part of this intimate project, it is necessary above all to come to a better awareness of Mary, this forgotten one. The questionable advances of a theology which has been invaded by human sciences, by philosophies which are hardly compatible with Christianity, and by the influence of the masters of suspicion have effectively placed Mary on the sidelines. She is more removed from hearts and minds than she was during my childhood. Certainly, the Council correctly disposed of a number of excesses. It's not a question of returning to them, to the detriment of Christian balance and of ecumenism. But too often, the baby has been thrown out with the bath water. Along with the abuses of the past, Mary, our beloved mother, and her very virginity have been dismissed. In order to rediscover her, it will be necessary to get beyond the ideologies and false cultural tendencies which have made of Mary an unreal figure and, in effect, a myth. It will be important for us to rediscover her as she really is: such as she is in herself when viewed from the aspect of eternity.

We will rediscover her first of all in history, for she is certainly an historical personage: her existence and her life's history are certainly incontestable when ordinary methods of history are applied to her: methods such as those by which we are able to have certain knowledge regarding the essential aspects of the life of Julius Caesar and Alexander the Great, of Plato, or even of Socrates — this in spite of the artificial aspects of the literature concerning this philosopher.

I have already established the scientific controls of this historical approach in *The truth of Christmas beyond the myths, the gospels of the infancy of Christ,* St Bede's Press, 1985. I will not erect this historical scaffolding once again, but instead will set forth directly and concretely the story of Mary just as I have studied it during a period of forty years of patient scholarly approaches coming together from a variety of types of research: an ordinary story externally, an extraordinary one internally.

Making mention of this appears to be quite necessary, since a persistent religious deformation is frequently being repeated in exegesis as well as in catechesis: little importance should be given to the history of Jesus, and *a fortiori*, to the story of Mary; we don't know anything about it but this is really of no importance. What is important is the symbolic and theological truth which the earliest Christian generations painstakingly concocted. Little importance need be accorded the Jesus of history; the Christ of faith is sufficient for us. Little importance need be accorded the Mary of history; only her symbolic truth is important for our faith. This dissociation creates an uncertitude and a very unfortunate clouding over of our knowledge of Christ and of Mary. If, history could have proven (as has frequently been attempted in various ways) that Joan of Arc was only a myth, this heroine (universally beloved of Frenchmen, from communists to the extreme right — not to mention a number of English writers, such as Bernard Shaw) would lose all her human, national and Christian relevance. She would be no more than a mere literary fact. If this young girl had been burned at the stake only in the imagination of a good fourteenth-century storyteller, she would lose ninety per cent of her value, if not more.

The same could be said of Jesus and Mary if their image, from the point of view of faith, is dissociated from their historical reality.

Let us no longer say that the historical truth and uncertain history of Christ and his miracles are of little importance and that what really counts is meaning. With regard to everything which matters in our lives, be it money or love, we do not confuse illusion with truth: the cheque which clears and the cheque which bounces, fidelity and the deception of the cheat. Indifference to realities of faith translates into indifference to faith itself: to the effective encounter with God, with Christ, with Mary.

3 It is from these inescapable historical bases, the visible impact of the Incarnation, that dogma derives its meaning. This will be the subject of a third section.

4 But it is not merely a matter of knowing this Mary who loves us, we have to meet her: to discover her presence and her role in this consecration to God which is the essential business of our life. This will be the subject of the final chapter.

From diversity to unity

This book, focused in the most direct way possible upon Mary in her essential bonds with Christ, does not ignore the diversity of views which have been expressed over the centuries — for the Virgin Mary always surpasses us, and each period discovered her by means of its own particular antennae and sensibilities, but not without distortion. We will sift through these fleeting peculiarities, in order to present as direct as possible a knowledge of the Mother of God to our world of harried humankind.

Each age has formed its own particular image of Mary; that of the fathers of the Church is not that of the Middle Ages; that of the icons is not that of our cathedrals. But watch out! Do not say: the Virgin is only what we make of her by virtue of our own particular culture and imagination. No, she is indeed this woman of Nazareth, who became the unique Mother of Christ. And the diversity of images is one of our means of expression. These always partial and imperfect modalities ignore her and take her up again, even to the point of a number of regrettable distortions and betrayals which we must correct and go beyond; the sentimental dramatisation of the baroque period and the abstract stylisation of our era. The mother of the Lord surpasses all the means of our expression. But it is certainly she who inspires them and gives them their greatest verification. If pluralism exists, it is not in the person of Mary, but in the bankruptcy of these modes of expression: images and language.

What about ecumenism?

We should remember the reservations of our Protestant brothers, who accept with us the entirety of scripture, but who have often been shocked by the approximations, exaggerations and polarisations of many Catholic expressions.

I have remained in dialogue with other Christian confessions and believe that in spite of our historical differences, the Virgin, when properly understood, can only be a sign of unity. From the beginning and with all of her heart, she has only sought unity, like Christ, through Christ, in Christ. Her mission, from the time of the Incarnation in which she established the human bases for God's becoming man, has been to serve unity.

It is true that for a long time she has appeared as a sign of contradiction, but this is the result of misunderstandings which we have to go beyond and eliminate. We will not discuss them here, but this task of purification and of truth will continue to be ours with reference to the pluralism of the New Testament.

From biblical pluralism to confessional pluralism

Although there is no doctrinal expression in Mark, there are actually three different theological perspectives on Mary in the New Testament:

1 The vision of Paul (*Galatians 4:4*) regarding Christ born of woman, the means of his self-emptying (*kenosis*) in the Incarnation;

2 The soaring vision of John. The new focus of Christ on women culminates there in Mary;

3 The concrete and stimulating vision of *Luke 1-2*, the sole hagiographer of the New Testament, the one who introduces us to Peter, Paul, Stephen and other admirable models in the Acts of the Apostles. He is called the painter of Mary, for he knew how to paint her spiritual portrait with the essentials of her vocation and her unparalleled adventure with God.

These three visions coincide, in various degrees, with those of the three major Christian confessions:

1 Protestants continue the tradition of Paul, sober, anonymous, unencumbered, since the apostle finds his meaning and purpose through the risen Christ who had knocked him from his horse on the road to Damascus, rather than through the Incarnation, by which Mary had brought Christ into our midst. We should note particularly the insistence with which the encyclical of John Paul II adopts this pauline perspective by starting with *Galatians 4:4*. This is one of the ecumenical values of the encyclical.

2 The Orthodox continue the tradition of John, in the wake of his abrupt formula, the 'Word was made flesh'. The term *theotokos,* and the bright vision of the *aeiparthenos,* the ever-Virgin indissolubly present at the mysteries of Christ, has been derived from this.

3 Catholics find their place in the tradition of St Luke, who discovers in Mary a presence and a more personal model.

Election, selection and preferences are legitimate. They characterise the confessions like spiritual schools. But there is no need to limit oneself to one section of scripture, thereby excluding all the others. Ecumenism, moreover, has as its purpose to allow us to have access to biblical fullness, to Christian fullness, to the fullness of Revelation. The present work, which is being addressed essentially to Catholics in order to help them to live out the plan and purpose of the Holy Father, also seeks to help all persons of good will to discover this sister and this mother who is totally open to and at the disposal of so many of her orphaned children.

This work, which is essentially addressed to Catholics in order to help them implement the Pope's project should also assist non-Christians in understanding who this woman is: the best-known, the most often named, painted and sculpted of women whether in literature, the arts or human culture. She is not a dream or an artistic product, this number one superstar on whom so many current phantasms and bitter disappointments — even to the point of considering her to be a possessive Mother — have been projected. Mary is not a creation of the human mind. She has inspired artists because she exists. She inspires by *what* she is. This is one of the fundamental perceptions which this book seeks to re-establish in a civilisation shot through with a philosophy of idealism which reduces so many things to subjectivity. Mary is neither a product nor an object for consumption, but an historical personage, a living and loving person, a mother, our mother, whom we really need to get to know better. Because everyone who has come to know her during the last two thousand years can only be thankful for having made her acquaintance.

1

WHY THIS YEAR OF GRACE WITH MARY?

The surprise of 1 January 1987
The announcement of this year in union with Mary was certainly a surprise.

Contrary to normal practice, the press had not received any advance notice of this announcement. (There was an embargo up until the date of the authorised release of this news.) This is quite rare although not unique. It happens when an unforeseen inspiration obliges the Pope to go full steam ahead. Such was the case with the extraordinary synod — convoked to celebrate the twentieth anniversary of the end of the Second Vatican Council, in 1985.

On the morning of 1 January 1987 I concelebrated, in a community, with a highly placed prelate of the French Church. He told me the news in confidence . . . the news 'fell', some hours later, from the mouth of the Holy Father in his homily during the Mass of Mary Mother of God, in St Peter's Basilica in Rome. John Paul II announced it by means of a prayer addressed to Mary:

> You are Blessed, You who believed (*Luke 1:45*).
> The Church fixes her eyes on You as upon its proper model. . . at this time when she looks forward to celebrating the advent of the third millennium of the Christian era, and in order to prepare for this, the Church . . . wishes to celebrate a year especially dedicated to You, a Marian Year . . ., a year in which every Diocese will celebrate in its own way in order to plumb the depths of your mystery and to promote devotion to you, a renewed commitment of union with the will of God, in accordance with the example offered by You, servant of the Lord.

This announcement gave me just enough time to phone in a preliminary article to the *Figaro,* in order to explain the meaning of this unexpected news.

The refusal of a bimillennium

The announcement was totally unexpected, for a 'Marian' Year had been requested of the Pope right from the start of his pontificate. And he had refused it. Petitions which had been brought by various Italian groups and promoted by the *Collegamento Mariano,* a powerful movement of all the associations and institutions dedicated to the Blessed Virgin over which Bishop Franzi presides, had as their purpose the celebration of the 'bimillennium of the birth of Mary'. According to tradition, (based upon the age for marriage in Palestine) the promoters suggested celebrating this anniversary some fifteen years before the bimillennium of the birth of Christ.

But the date of this birth, calculated by Dionysius Exiguus at the beginning of the seventh century, is only an approximation and the chronology is uncertain. The majority of today's exegetes teach that Jesus was born between four and seven years 'before Christ' for it was 'during the time of Herod' (*Matthew 2* and *Luke 1, 2*) and according to our dating, Herod would die four or five years before the birth of Jesus Christ. Moreover, an Anglo-Saxon view, based upon coinage and the comparison of various calendars of the period, placed the death of Herod in the year one before Jesus Christ. This option, (which needs to be very loudly and soundly qualified) has scarcely been taken into consideration. However it has received some support at the Hebrew University in Jerusalem on the basis of its being closer to archaeological data. Recent promoters of the bimillennium hold to the more common opinion. And thus it was that the Republic of San Marino celebrated this anniversary from 8 December, 1979 to 8 December, 1980.

Increasing requests to extend this initiative to the universal Church seemed to find a favourable reception on the part of a Pope who had come from Poland: hadn't this Church achieved its marvellous renewal by preparing for the millennium of the faith? The response of John Paul II was negative. Why? Because the Secretariat of State had already given a negative response in the name of Paul VI, on 13 December 1976. A precedent had already been set and this would hold. As early as 1884, Leo XIII had refused Cardinal Haynald, Archbishop of Budapest, the possibility of celebrating the nineteenth centenary of the birth of Mary. This was done because of the uncertainty of the dates.

This chronological uncertainty seemed to have been overcome, for Pius XI side-stepped the problem by celebrating the nineteenth centenary of the Redemption in 1933. He cut short the interminable circular discussions concerning the birth of Christ and held to the conventional understanding of the dating of the birth of Christ:

— Christ was 'about thirty years of age' at the beginning of his ministry, according to *Luke 3:23*.
— According to the most common opinion, this ministry lasted some three years.
— The nineteenth centenary was therefore celebrated in 1900 + 33 = 1933.

For the bimillennium of Mary, the Secretariat of State stuck to the arguments of Leo XIII and Paul VI. On 26 July, 1982, in the name of John Paul II, it responded:

> After a new examination by competent departments, His Holiness has confirmed, in accordance with the will of his predecessor Paul VI, that he does not foresee an opportunity to agree with the said proposal.

The intense campaign that had been launched with petitions was immediately called off out of perfect obedience.

An Advent with Mary

It was therefore quite a surprise when, on 15 August 1983 at Lourdes, John Paul II declared, during his homily: 'Wouldn't it be opportune to celebrate the second millennium of the birth of Mary?'

Was the Pope annulling the negative response of the Secretariat of State? Father G. Felci, a Capuchin, Director of the Marian Missions of Loreto, who had campaigned for this cause, inaugurated a new international campaign of petitions which was well received at the International Marian Congress of Malta.

On 31 August 1983 *L'Osservatore Romano*[2] seemed to support this new initiative. The article announced 'a world day in honour of Mary' to be celebrated in Rome on the following 2 October, at the sanctuary of *Divino Amore* and it linked this celebration to the bimillennium.

But on 30 September 1983, just before this Roman celebration, there was a new article in *L'Osservatore Romano* entitled 'Mary at the Advent of the year 2000', which confirmed the status quo.

There would be neither a document of the Holy See nor an official celebration of the bimillennium by a Holy Year, on the scale of the universal Church. What the Holy Father recommended to local Churches and to various religious families was to prepare for the year 2000 in union with Mary by means of a long 'Advent' with her in preparation for the bimillennium of Christ. Thus several churches celebrated a year of the 'bimillennium of Mary' (the Latin Patriarchate of Jerusalem: 8 September 1984 — 8 September 1985); the Philippines (9 December 1985 — 8 December 1986). John Paul II's plan is therefore to prepare for the 2000th anniversary of the coming of Christ with Mary, without focusing upon the anniversary of her birth. This reflects his concern to go beyond pre-conciliar triumphalism for the sake of a greater interiorisation and more sustained effort. He chose to do so by means of this year dedicated to Mary, from 7 June 1987 to 15 August 1988.

Moreover this pope, who came from Poland and who lives intensely his mission as a man who is hinged between east and west, between Christian east and west, has chosen, in preference to a bimillennium of Mary at the beginning of the eighties, the year of the millennium of Christianity in Russia: Kiev, 1988. Undoubtedly he has, in this particular decision, a plan which he probably confided to Our Lady. Is it the new consecration of Russia for which certain groups have been hoping? Is it a celebration of Mary with the Patriarch of Moscow? Or is it something else? In so difficult an area as this we must be on our guard against premature conclusions.

Immediate and profound reasons for this decision

What, then, are the reasons for this mature decision?

Undoubtedly there is a concern to arrive at a proper termination of the second millennium in this its final century, tormented by the first two world wars and threatened by a third which would be deadly for humanity. There is also the need to step back, enlarge upon the perspective from God's point of view and consider his designs for the salvation of the world. But the perspective of an 'Advent with Mary', up to the year 2000, which emerged in the homily at Lourdes, reappears with a certain amount of insistence in the announcement of 1 January 1987. The Church, the Pope stated, turns towards Mary,

> in order to celebrate the advent of the third millennium of the Christian era, in order better to prepare itself for this event, (with the one who) was the providential instrument which the Son of God used in order to become son of man and give a beginning to a new era . . .

And further on:

> As we cross over into this new millennium, we must always learn a great deal more from you about how to be Christian.

Using contemporary needs as his primary focus, the Pope wishes to refashion an authentically Christian Church and world so that Christ will be born again into our world. What really counts are these profound and lasting reasons which are the subject of this book. As for special reasons, the Pope, wishing to be in solidarity with his predecessors, does not wish to fashion a Marian Year in accordance with a preconciliar, solemn, triumphalistic style. He hopes for something less external and much deeper.

Is this why he extended this 'year' to fourteen months and eight days? Perhaps. But it was especially in order to begin this year on Pentecost, a year which will finish on the Feast of the Assumption, 1988. He thus refers Mary to the Holy Spirit, since on that day there came upon her and upon the Church a new plentitude (*Acts 1:14; 2*), for, as Christian tradition tells us, it is through the Holy Spirit that it is primarily and above all appropriate for Mary to bear the title 'Mother of the Church'.

> The Mother of the Universal Church is the grace of the Holy Spirit. Mother is the Holy Church, Mother par excellence is said to be Mary, the Mother of the Lord . . . and she seems to be Mother of the Church, for certainly being Mother of the Head it follows that she is to be understood as Mother of the body. The Church is Mother of Mary and Mary Mother of the Church, (*Distinctiones monasticae,* Editions Pitras, *Spicilegium solesmense 3,* pp. 130-131)

We are not dealing with a year focused solely upon Mary, but one opened totally to the Holy Spirit who is the secret of Mary. And John Paul II gave pride of place to the Holy Spirit at the beginning of the homily in which he announced a year dedicated to Mary. The Spirit is the source 'of Christian liberty and of liberation', he stressed, in order to show his positive concern to promote a new theology of liberation which goes beyond the ambiguities (*L'Osservatore Romano,* p. 5, col 1).

Perhaps also, he wants to profit from this year in order to launch once again the plan for the consecration of the world which has been considered from the time of Pius XII. This hypersecularised, atheistic, materialistic world of ours has an urgent need to rediscover God by consecrating itself to him.

The basic reasons of John Paul II are linked to his personal experience and to that of several particular churches, which the Pope, in accordance with the constant strand of tradition, desires to share with the universal Church.

The experience of John Paul II

The fundamental experience of the future Pope, Karol Wojtyla, is to be found in his youth, when as a student he served his time as a worker in the factories of Solvay. He brought with him the *Treatise of True Devotion* by Grignion de Montfort which he read during breaks, and his copy of this little book is still stained with chemical particles. Karol's heart was enlightened by the book and this was an important step in his ascent toward the priesthood and his entire future, which was dedicated to Our Lady. This is why his first words as Pope, on the Piazza of St Peter, were addressed to our Lady. His shield, which is located under the initial of Mary, is taken from de Montfort: *totus tuus:* everything for you.

The experience of Poland

Karol Wojtyla preceded the Primate of Poland, Stefan Wyszynski, who, ten years later, made the same consecration. It was 8 December 1953. He was under arrest, cut off from the bishops and his people, reduced to intense prayer. Such a strong man was frustrated in every manner of activity. Refusing to despair under these desperate circumstances, he made his consecration: 'For three weeks, I prepared myself for this day. Through the intermediary of the best of all mothers, I made myself a slave of Christ.'

He was so bold as to employ this term which was used by the apostle Paul: *'slave of Christ'*. 'Slavery' is a sordid and hateful word which describes the alienation of a human person for the benefit of a creature who sets himself up as God and as an abusive master. But this word 'slave' has an altogether different sense, if it is referred, in total liberty, to the transcendent God. God does not alienate. The creator does not enslave. He creates. He gives existence itself to us. He gives us our very liberty, including an absolute capacity for turning ourselves away from or against the Creator. If we use this negative power in which we imagine ourselves to be creator, we are the creators of our own evil and our own destruction. We can do all this, but God alone can liberate us from sin. To say that one is a slave of God is to recognise that we owe everything to him, starting with our very existence and freedom. This is a profoundly upsetting and misunderstood truth in which life finds its meaning and its purpose.

Moreover, God creates out of love, and authentic love is never alienation, even if the language of love sometimes professes slavery with respect to the person loved. There is no slavery when there is reciprocity in love.

This profound experience was to be extended by Wyszynski to his people. From the residence in which he was under house arrest, he secretly sent an Act of Consecration for Poland to be read at the national sanctuary of Our Lady of Czestochowa: 'If there is no bishop present, let a priest read it. If there is no priest present, let a layman or sacristan read it, but let it be read', he insisted.

Thus there began the steady and irresistible rise of the three Ws: Wyszynski, Wojtyla and Walesa.

— Wyszynski methodically re-fashioned the faith, families, catechesis, seminaries and an elite of priests and bishops, all in accordance with Mary's will.

— Wojtyla was one of this new generation, one whose age and breadth of vision would furnish the youngest pope of the twentieth century, the first Polish pope. The faith of Poland, which had been taken for granted for a long time, was now seen to be exemplary, more strongly and authentically Catholic than it had ever been.

— Walesa then came along. He manifested a new dimension of this vigour. The Polish Church which the socio-cultural intelligentsia had depicted as being priest-ridden and authoritarian had fostered the creativity of an independent laity. We understand why Walesa, however respectful of the atheism of certain of his fellow union members, dared to wear his rosary around his neck during the meetings in which he defended the first and only union which had been born in a Marxist regime.

Amazed at this 'Polish miracle' which I had seen rising in the east in the course of a dozen trips there, going back as far as the sixties, I once asked Cardinal Wyszynski, shortly before his death, what his secret was. He did not hesitate: 'It is the Blessed Virgin', he responded, showing me the treatise of Grignion de Montfort *(True Devotion)*, which he kept on his prie-dieu.

The experience of other Churches

This fruitful experiment is not peculiar to Poland. It has succeeded, to different degrees, in other places where it has been attempted. Portugal, where the plan for the consecration of the world, taken up by Pius XII, Paul VI and John Paul II, began, has escaped world war and the threatening onslaught of Marxism.

Italy, which made its national consecration on 13 September 1959, at the end of the Eucharistic Congress, and which celebrated the twenty-fifth anniversary of this consecration, has shown greater resistance to post-conciliar drift than other western countries, as regards seminaries, Sunday attendance, Christian creativity and popular religion.

At the beginning of his pontificate, John Paul II was invited to renew this consecration to Mary which Lucy, the visionary of Fatima, judged still to fall short of the requests of Our Lady: she felt that the participation by bishops was inadequate, and regretted diplomatic concessions to Russia.

The attempt on his life on 13 May 1982, the anniversary of the first apparition of Fatima, and the manner in which he almost miraculously escaped death, focused the Pope's attention on the urgency of Mary's demand. In the Gemelli Hospital in Rome, at the beginning of his convalescence, he was urged by a friend of his youth, Dr Wanda Poltawska, to re-read the message of Fatima. The following year, he renewed, in thanksgiving, the consecration of the world and Russia at Fatima itself. He received Lucy for about twenty minutes. And as she was still not satisfied at the bishops and the entire Church not having taken up the consecration, he renewed a second time this consecration with the bishops of the entire world gathered together in synod on the occasion of the closing of the Holy Year, 24 and 25 March 1984, the Feast of the Annunciation.

A further spiritual adventure concerns the people of the Philippines. Whereas in many countries and dioceses the consecration requested by the Holy Father was reduced to a number of formal acts which were often quite low key, Cardinal Sin, Archbishop of Manila, committed all of his people to it with great vigour. Under an oppressive dictatorship, which was in the process of becoming even more severe and in which the misery of the poor had increased significantly, this celebration was accompanied by fasts in order to feed those who were dying of hunger. In the end, faith, mutual assistance and justice triumphed for this generous people.

In order to continue and deepen this spiritual movement, Cardinal Sin decided to celebrate the bimillennium of the birth of the Virgin, from 8 December 1983 to 8 December 1984 and he did so using prayer and fasting. This fervent year allowed for the peaceful return to democracy. At the very time when President Marcos invalidated the elections and proclaimed himself the winner against Cory Aquino, the widow of his rival whom he had assassinated, the Cardinal (in agreement with a courageous minister) asked the people to take to the streets of the capital. An immense crowd camped out, night and day, on the Grand Plaza and in neighbouring streets for a period of forty-eight hours. They did this in a completely peaceful manner, for they had become capable of peace, through prayer and fasting. Not one stone was hurled against the crowd or the armoured vehicles. Instead, young girls offered flowers to the soldiers and this resulted in the army's rallying around those who were looking for justice.

This is not the place to comment on the difficult national and political adventure of the Philippines. Despite her triumph, Cory Aquino, who had prayed and fasted like the rest, is caught in a vice between the communist guerrillas and the forces of the Right who threaten her. Those who predicted her rapid loss of control are astonished that she has obtained a ceasefire from the guerrillas and put down the Right's first attempt to gain power. Her line of national reconciliation remains intact despite difficult political problems.

What we need to stress here is the spiritual renewal of a people dedicated to Mary, through mutual assistance, solidarity, generosity, a concern for justice and the common good and the national reconciliation which she inspired. Isn't it precisely here under the aegis of Mary and her Magnificat that the theology of liberation has given its best proofs: 'He put down the mighty from their throne and has exalted the humble'?

These occasions of spiritual renewal transcend the politics of right and left. Consecrated Poland is acting out its drama with an all-powerful atheistic materialism, and its leader has no other concern than to obtain an audience with the Pope in order to attain a semblance of legitimacy once again. But in the Philippines, when faced with a dictatorship of another type, the faith revealed itself as an irresistible force in favour of liberty, democracy and popular unity.

The overview of some of these trouble-spots, which we could have enlarged upon, shows how the marian year decided upon by John Paul II will prolong the great plan of the consecration of the world which has been in the process of being realised since Pius XII. What John Paul II has focused upon, what he proposes, is that this consecration become effective. The fact that three successive popes have renewed it on eight occasions is not sufficient, for a pontifical action remains formal and devotional. The consecration must become real in the heart of everyone. This is one of the ends of this year with Mary.

Towards the bimillennium of Christ

There is also another reason: As we have said, John Paul II sees in this year a preparation for the bimillennium of the birth of Christ in the year 2000. He refers prophetically to this date, on which he will have reached the age of eighty (28 May 2000). Placed at this particular juncture in history, he wants the third millennium to open, after the successive tragic shocks since the end of the eighteenth century, upon a renewal of faith and of the reign of Christ. Certainly, numbers such as the year 2000 are only symbols. But they speak to us. They are able to conjure up feelings of terror or hope: a terror going back to the year 1000, a hope for the year 2000.

To share once more, to launch once again, to spread even further the personal and community experiences of the Virgin, which have been mentioned in this chapter, to reactualise her presence in this world, to promote by her example and through her a consecration of the world, including Russia, to God as Saviour, to prepare in this way for the third millennium, such are the chief focuses of John Paul II's master plan.

In order to enter more effectively into this, let us come close to Our Lady, let us have a better understanding of who she is according to history and then according to dogma, which reveals to us the extraordinary position accorded by God to this humble woman of Palestine. Finally, let us learn how to rediscover the presence of this mother to whom Jesus has confided each and every one of us.

2

MARY IN OUR HISTORY: A GOSPEL PERSPECTIVE

Is it necessary to place faith and historical reality in opposition?

'Mary is a symbolic personage rather than an historical personage.' So declared a celebrated American Catholic exegete. Such is the fashion today. Religion and reality are dissociated as if faith belonged to the realm of dreams, as if the greatest good of the human being were subjectivity. This unreality is disastrous for our culture and ruinous for faith.

Mary in the history of the poor

What is true in this agnostic perspective of Mary is that this village girl from Nazareth in Galilee stems from the history of the poor, and the poor have no history. Even in the civil sector they have escaped history totally: they have disappeared without trace, like the flowers of springtime. For the poor were unlettered and such was probably the case with Mary. They left no writing and the history of the poor will only be written in heaven for our wonderment. Mary was dedicated and committed to those forgotten women of history, and exegetes who wish to make of her a pure symbol write, like J. McKenzie: 'The Virgin of history only deserves an embarrassed silence like the silence in which the mother of Abraham Lincoln lies buried' (*Concilium,* no 138, 1983, p. 160).

Truly, with the exception of Abraham Lincoln, the mothers of heroes are like queens, those who have the best chance of being preserved from oblivion. When the fruitful womb of the world of the poor produced a hero, his mother was able to enter into history. And such was the case with Mary, known as 'Mother of Jesus', this other poor man who escaped the silence of history only just in time.

The gospels contain a quantity of straightforward specifics about Mary which permit us to know her as a real person, a person who cannot be erased from the map of history.

She came from Nazareth in Galilee. She bore the name Mary.

She was married to Joseph, an obscure descendant of David, a carpenter in the village. Her marriage (*gidusin:* a name which signifies sanctification) took place in two stages:

— The agreement, the contract *(erusin).*
— Then the cohabitation, the entrance of the wife into the home of the husband *(nisuin).*

It is between these two stages that there was produced in Mary that out-of-sequence, unexpected event which will be considered further on in this work.

Daily life

We could retrace, in accordance with the methods of the new kind of historical research, the infancy of a little Jewish girl in the city known as Nazareth, her marriage arranged by the clan, the daily life of the 'Holy Family', with its household utensils and the tools of the carpenter, at a time in which the simple tool was the only aid for the hand which by itself provided all the necessary energy for the task.

It was an austere time: not under-development but pre-development, a more tragic situation, with frequent and unrelenting famines and without any possibility of convoys filled with assistance coming from all over the world.

Women's lives are always more continuously burdened than men's lives. At that time a woman was rough and ready to an extent that we can no longer imagine. Mary could not go to a baker in order to buy bread. She had to start from scratch to prepare the grain by winnowing it. She could not go into a chain store to buy clothing. She had to prepare the wool and do the weaving herself. There were no matches. She had to tend the fire, gather the wood, a task that would continue for women of Nazareth up until the beginning of this century. If, as a carpenter, Joseph could lighten her burden in this respect, Mary certainly still had to do just as much as other women did.

Mary was pious, she prayed. Although, in Judaism the synagogue is basically a man's domain, women could look on from the place specially reserved for them, away from where the men were seated. Luke attests that Mary had a very profound knowledge of the Scriptures. She undoubtedly received this by means of oral tradition since it is not likely that a village girl would have known how to read. At a time when libraries were empty, memories were full.

The Holy Family made a pilgrimage to Jerusalem each year (*Luke 2:41*) in accordance with the law (*Exodus 23:14-17; 34:22-23; Deuteronomy 16:10*).

Two of Mary's pilgrimages are known to us: the one when Jesus was twelve years of age (*Luke 2:41*) and the one when he was thirty-three years of age where she found him on the gruesome hill of Golgotha (*John 19:25-27*).

Portrait of Mary

The gospels are all almost silent regarding Mary. Only Luke gives us a glimpse of her spiritual make-up. The cultivated doctor, using the new methods through which the Greeks had become the fathers of historical writing, had inquired among 'eyewitnesses' (*1:2*). It was not difficult to find them in the Jerusalem community that he visited several times (*Acts 11:17-28*) according to the western text, and *21:12-17*. He quotes witnesses of the infancy: neighbours of John the Baptist who 'pondered these words and events in their hearts' (*Luke 1:6*); and Mary, who did likewise, according to the refrain which appears at two key moments in his gospel:

— at the end of the account of Christmas (*2:19*): 'She treasured all these things and pondered them in her heart';
— at the end of the entire gospel of the infancy (*2:51*): 'His mother stored up all these things in her heart'.

The principal phrase, 'store up' is nuanced by two prefixes:

— She 'gathered' them, collated them, gathered them in (the Greek verb *SYNterein*, *Luke 2:19*).
— She analysed them, maintained them, and diligently preserved them (the Greek verb *DIAterein, Luke 2:51*).
— She contrasted or compared them, *(symballousa)* as *Luke 2:19* indicates. This Greek word, belonging to the word 'symbol', signifies the comparison of signs and memories from which light and meaning spring forth. *Luke 1-2*, the ultimate expression of these memories, confirms that they were indeed a lively and contemplative comparison of the events of the life of Christ with scripture. This account is shot through with biblical allusions showing that the coming of Jesus fulfilled all of the Scriptures. This comparison *(midrash)* was the process of Jewish prayer and exegesis in vogue at that time. The coming of Christ had in some way brought about a return to it. Previously it was scripture which enlightened

the event. Now it is the Christ event which enlightens all of scripture.

The account of the Annunciation is therefore the account of Mary's vocation. She alone knew this event. She alone was able to tell us of it. She had moulded it spontaneously in accordance with the style and the forms of biblical tradition, with a unique intensity causing them to burst forth periodically, giving them a meaning which was without precedent (René Laurentin, *The Truth of Christmas Beyond the Myths,* pp. 14-87).

We can therefore construct a twofold history of Mary:

— A history of her daily life according to the methods of the new history in order to attain — albeit tentatively — an understanding of the daily material and spiritual aspects of her life as one of the poor. (This remains to be done, but this is really not the right place.)
— A more classical history of the events of her life — for even within the rough outline of her daily life, we can see that Mary lived out a unique adventure. It was in this backwater and little-noticed town that the new and fundamental relation of God's love for men was being sketched out and this was not uneventful, as the gospels report.

We have a fragmentary knowledge of these events precisely because of Christ. Mary's proper role has quite rightfully been snatched from oblivion. In places where her name figures, it sometimes assumes an important place, at other times a secondary and even insignificant one (*Mark 3:20*).

These events need to be verified with the seriousness which is brought to bear upon authenticating family events — not with the systematic suspicion of a King Lear or the rationalist masters who have taught us the art of playing down, *a priori*, the divine and holy foundations of our history.

Mary's youth

The gospels teach us nothing of Mary's childhood. We can only resort to imagination and the less controllable revelations of the apocryphal writings and private revelations concerning her life: Maria d'Agreda, Katharina Emmerich, Maria Valtorta and others who seem to have had her life pass before their eyes like a film. In varying degrees, their revelations are akin to the

Protoevangelium of James, an apocryphal gospel without *historical value*. I do not say they are without *value*.

The *Protoevangelium of James* testifies not only to great fervour towards Mary, but also to a profound insight into her holiness and her virginity. Yet, in spite of its antiquity (the middle of the second century), it shows (unlike our gospels), a tremendous ignorance regarding the Jewish customs and laws which were operative in the temple in Jerusalem. It is totally unlikely that a little girl of three years of age could have been reared there — let alone in the holy of holies, reserved for priests on solemn occasions. If the liturgy celebrates the Presentation of Mary (21 November), it is because this symbolic account signifies the marvellous gift that Mary made of herself at the awakening of her conscience, she whom (as the dogmatic section of this book explains) God had preserved from every sin. But the Immaculate Conception, hinted at in the *Protoevangelium of James,* is not dependent upon history written on the strength of testimony.

This is one of the weaknesses of the revealed lives written by the three mystics cited above. They are often quite chatty and free-flowing, rich in the bright contemplation of their authors. But the emergence of episodes from the *Protoevangelium of James* seems quite obvious there. And the differences between these lives, their points of friction with historical data warn us that they are quite weak and untrustworthy. If their insights sometimes square with reality, it is generally impossible to sort out to what extent the account proceeds from a revelation or from the creative imagination of these women who are endowed with marvellous writing skills as well as a rare fervour and devotion. They have not written a more accurate and more complete super-gospel than the original gospel but a fragile complement; and the historian lacks the means to sort out, from these minerals, those historical nuggets which are genuine.

The success of these revealed lives is due in part to a lack of appreciation of the richness of the gospels, obscured by reductionistic exegesis. It is a reaction of fervent contemplation against the deadly dissection by the scribes and doctors of yesterday and today.

Mary's marriage

The first event in the life of Mary which is mentioned by the gospels is her marriage. When she received from God her vocation as Mother of God she was *emnesteumene,* married or affianced, but we should be hesitant in translating it thus since our word 'betrothal' does not take Jewish customs into consideration. *Emnesteumene* signifies the first phase of the marriage, the agreement and not the cohabitation which seals the marriage after a more or less prolonged period. *Luke 2:4* still employs this word at a time in which cohabitation takes place. He does this in order to suggest the non-consummation of the marriage.

The Jewish practices have, moreover, influenced ecclesiastical law: canonists distinguish the *ratum* (the ratified marriage) and the *consummatum* (consummated by sexual union). The Church can dissolve a ratified marriage, but not a consummated marriage which is irreversible (except where the necessary consent was not present from the start and this would invalidate the marriage). If Joseph had separated from Mary, according to his first plan (*Matthew 1:19*), this would have been a divorce, a repudiation.

What, then, was the marriage of Joseph and Mary? Pious, sentimental or psychoanalytic imagination has given itself free rein regarding the love of Joseph and of Mary, each coloured by their particular fantasies and subjectivity.

Whereas the apocryphal gospels depicted Joseph as an old man of advanced age, chosen as the protector of the Virgin, contemporary people have reacted tit-for-tat by imagining a marriage of love with all the concomitant arousals and stirrings of heart and of sexuality.

The gospels distance themselves from all of that. They teach us only two things:

1. At that time (as was still the case in France in the nineteenth century and during the early decades of the twentieth century), marriage was, as it still is among many people in Africa or elsewhere, a family affair.[4] Familial experience takes responsibility forthrightly and jointly for projects of future marriage. The family acts in much the same way as a village of fishermen which pools its resources in order to construct and launch a boat which is not going to capsize. It was therefore the clan of Nazareth which had arranged and prepared for this marriage in its first stage. The states of soul of both spouses and their reactions are not known to us.
2. Luke only specifies (from a trustworthy source) a single fact

(which some people have attempted to play down by every possible means, over the last two centuries and especially during this century). Mary had decided in her heart to devote her life exclusively to God, who was to be for her a love that would not be shared. Hence we understand her objection when she receives the glorious promise that she will be mother of the Messiah: indeed, even more, mother of the Son of God.

How can this be done since I have no knowledge of man?

Knowledge is meant in the sexual sense: 'Adam knew his wife and she conceived and bore Cain' (then Abel, then Seth: *Genesis 4:1, 25*).

It has been said: 'This resolve of Mary is unlikely, anachronistic'. A young girl of this period could only think of marriage and not of virginity. If, by constraint or illness she could not marry, she had no other resource at her disposal than to 'weep for her virginity', her lack of fulfilment, like the daughter of Jephtah (*Judges 11:37-38*).

But at Qumran and elsewhere, some groups of Essenes, including a community of 'aged virgins' about whom Philo Judaeus speaks (*De Vita Contemplativa,* no. 68) practised religious celibacy. This was, it is true, in a ritual perspective of legal purity but also of liturgical openness to all sacrifices. A half century later, the apostle Paul presents without any apology the situation of virgins as being more normal and preferable to marriage: 'He who marries his fiancée is doing well, and he who does not, better still' (*1 Corinthians 7:38*).

What the Christian communities discovered so quickly, Mary — chosen and loved by God, preserved from all sin, — embraced, most appropriately, forty years ahead of time. The scientific genius of certain scholars knows how to discover and impose new upsetting and unsuspected truths. Couldn't the religious genius of this poor young girl have invented what Luke tells us in so obvious a fashion? In so obvious and clear a fashion, that up to and including Harnack, reductionistic criticism has found no means to eliminate the embarrassment caused by this text other than to declare it to be unauthentic — the very thing which scientific criticism (textual and internal) has definitively excluded!

Without any despisal of marriage, any unhealthy frigidity or inhibition, some young people, boys and girls, even in our own day decide to go against the current because of a singular attraction to God. They choose to belong exclusively to him and to consecrate their lives to him, renouncing the need for their own goods and the values of this world, with its riches, power and human love (human *eros*).

Up until recent times, some young girls who had expressed this intention were often hindered from doing so. Their families imposed marriage upon them. There are several examples of this in the annals of sanctity. Such was the case with Sister Yvonne Aimée in 1920. She wanted to be a religious but her mother considered her best prepared for marriage and sought to have her viewpoint endorsed by her daughter's spiritual directors. Like a good mother, she began to introduce her to young men who would be, according to the bourgeois custom of the day, suitable marriage partners for her. But faced with these ridiculous candidates who were so foreign both to her humanity and her ideals, she preferred to choose secretly for herself the one whom she esteemed most among her friends. And when her decisive mystical encounter with Christ convinced both her directors and herself that she belonged radically to God alone, the young man who was so enamoured of her had a difficult time coping with this fact.

For Mary, marriage had its own particular role to play as a normal environment for the human education of the Son of God with mother and (adoptive) father, in a profound and tender union, in a life devoted to God.

In the light of these sketchy references, this is about all that one can say of the marriage of Mary. When speaking of Mary this biblical data can be respected without denigrating her.

I have dwelt on this point at a time when a certain Catholic exegete has made a great deal out of examining (with impartiality) three hypotheses in which he finds seeming equal merit: was the mother of Jesus a virgin, married or an adultress (like Mary Magdalene)?[5]

I admire the courageous and dizzying holiness of Mary Magdalene. Thérèse of Lisieux makes a great case for a prostitute who, out of love of God, would die on the very day of her conversion. But this holiness is different, a holiness in which the power of all-merciful love shines forth, different from the holiness of Mary in whom that love's power is directed towards another function right at the beginning of salvation: Mary's holiness had to be a flawless germ.

Theology and exegesis should not confuse everything — their function is to serve historical truth and the truth of God's plans as they have been transmitted accurately to us by reliable witnesses.

The vocation (Luke 1:28-38)

We shall now look more closely at Mary's vocation which Luke intended to base upon his experience with eyewitnesses (*Luke 1:2*). He has given us an account of this under a form which is both astonishingly sober and quite to the point. The revelation which is going to overturn her life and the future of the world comes from a mysterious messenger of God whom she recognises as Gabriel, the angel of the prophecy of the seventy weeks (*Daniel 7-9*). His message is contained in six verses which are punctuated by two responses from Mary:

— a demand for an explanation (*Luke 1:34*);

— her consent, her unreserved *fiat* (*1:38*).

(I have already commented on this scene in *The Truth of Christmas Beyond the Myths, The Gospels of the Infancy of Christ*. My purpose here will be to sort out what is essential.)

The traditional literary model in which Mary conveyed her memories is less an account of *birth* than an account of vocation. If the announcement to Zechariah of John the Baptist's forthcoming birth (*Luke 1:4-25*) is typically a birth account according to the model of the birth of Samson in *Judges 13*, the announcement to Mary is said to resemble that of Gideon (*Judges 6*). Like him ('valiant warrior'), she receives a new name. But it is a name of grace and a declaration of love coming from on high. 'Rejoice, *Kecharitomene*' (*Luke 1:28).*

This word (a perfect participle of *charitoo:* to love, to pamper, to favour) signifies the object par excellence of all of God's love, of his inclination, of his gracious favour, of his predilection. It is untranslatable. We can say 'Full of grace', or simply 'Beloved of God'.

God chose this Beloved in order to make of himself a man. The messenger first said to her: 'Rejoice'. This is the key word by which the prophets announced the future messianic joy — notably *Zephaniah 3:14-17*, which the announcement to Mary takes up in order to reveal its immediate fulfilment.

The prophet's announcement to Israel Zephaniah 3:14-17	**Announcement to Mary Luke 1:28-33**
Shout for joy [*chaire*] daughter of Zion. . .	Rejoice You who enjoy God's favour!
Yahweh is king among you [literally 'in your bowels']	The Lord is with you. . .
Zion have no fear. . .	Mary, do not be afraid. . .
Yahweh your God is there with you	Look! You are to conceive in your womb and bear a son and you must name him
the warrior – Saviour	Jesus. . . son of the Most High. . . He will rule. . .

The prophecy from the time of the exile is realised in Mary. What the prophet announced regarding the future of the daughter of Zion (a fictitious personalisation of Israel, as little Marianne with the phrygian bonnet personifies France), is what the message of God announces to Mary here and now. This will not be the coming again of the glory of God which mysteriously shines forth from the Ark of the Covenant. This glory of God is going to be incarnated in humility. Mary will conceive *a son*. And this son will be called Son of the Most High (*Luke 1:2*).

In the cultural context of that time, the expression 'He will be called' does not relativise the name but amplifies it: He will *be* and in addition will be *called*, that is to say *recognised in truth,* as Son of God. This is shocking news which Mary receives, in a flash of lightning at the centre of her life.

It is only after having declared that her son will be the *Son of the Most High*, God himself, that the messenger declares him to be *Messiah*, much less son of David than *Son of God* (a title of great priority: repeated in *1, 32a* and *35b*). The messenger continues:

> The Lord God will give him the throne of his ancestor David; he will rule over the House of Jacob for ever and his reign will have no end.

Joseph, the husband, mentioned at the beginning of the

narrative, has disappeared. This announcement is not addressed to him. It is to Mary alone that the announcement is made and the name of Joseph will not reappear until the birth of Christ. He was present because of Mary, 'married to a man named "Joseph" '. He will no longer figure in the narrative except to be excluded by Mary's negative statement: 'I have no knowledge of man' (*Luke 1:34*).

She who is 'married to a man' has decided 'not to know man' according to a singular intention inspired in her by God himself. But how, then, does God invite her now to be a mother?

Mary dares to question, to object. Zechariah, the priest, who had received in the course of his priestly functions in the temple a message similar to that given to Mary — the announcement of the birth of a son in his old age — also dared to present an objection: 'How am I to know this?'

> How can I know this? I am an old man and my wife is getting on in years (*Luke 1:18*).

But Zechariah was punished for his audacity, was struck speechless for having dared to put God to the test. Will it be the same for Mary? No, the mother of the Son of God has a right to speak up which was refused the priest. This poor young girl is certainly higher than the priest. She has a right to a response, for her objection comes from God himself. And the messenger's response constitutes the high point of the message. Here again, the explanation is given to Mary in the only language she knows, that of the Bible. Thc response gives current value to another text (*Exodus* 40:35) in which God takes possession of the Ark of the Covenant constructed because of Moses' great concern. God twice manifested his presence there:

— above the Ark by means of the cloud (the *shekina*);
— inside it, by his resplendent glory.

The presence above signifies the transcendence of God. The glory within signifies his immanence.

Exodus 40:34
How God came into the ark

The cloud then covered the
Tent of Meeting [Tabernacle]
and the glory of Yahweh filled
the Dwelling

Luke 1:35
How God will come into Mary

The power of the Most High
will cover you with its shadow
And so the child will be holy,
and will be called Son of God.

(*cf. Numbers 16-22; 2 Chronicles 5:13-14*).

The presence of God is no longer luminously radiant as in the time of Moses, but it becomes a bodily birth: the Incarnation. The one who is going to be 'begotten' of Mary is indeed designated as 'Holy' ('God alone is Holy': *1 Samuel 2:2,* etc; cf, *The Truth of Christmas Beyond the Myths*), the Son of God will become the son of Mary.

Zechariah had asked God for a sign guaranteeing the unbelievable birth announced at his advanced age and he had no other sign than the punishment of being struck dumb. Mary, who has not asked for a sign, receives one: this marvellous birth by which her cousin Elizabeth, mother of John the Baptist, will be made so happy and joyful:

> Your cousin Elizabeth also, in her old age, has conceived a son and she whom people called barren is now in her sixth month, for nothing is impossible to God (*Luke 1:36*).

These words take up again the word of God to Sarah who became pregnant in her old age (*Genesis 18:14*). This essential and fundamental dialogue ends with the total consent of Mary. In contrast to the powerless gestures of Zechariah who had been struck dumb, she speaks up and concludes:

> You see before you the Lord's servant, let it happen to me as you have said, (*Luke 1:38*).

God addresses himself directly to Mary's freedom. She consents to God, to life, to salvation. She responds freely to love, by love, and we can be grateful to her for this, for her consent opens the way to the very foundation or basis of our salvation: the Incarnation. God does nothing in us without us.

Visit to her cousin Elizabeth

The Son of God therefore became son of Mary. Is Mary going to preserve this totally unexpected, this amazing grace for herself? No, she hastens to leave in order to share what is beyond measure. She is going to visit her cousin Elizabeth: to share the grace about which the angel has spoken to her. Mary left in haste, as *Luke 1:39* observes, towards the mountains of Judaea. For there is located the house of her cousin, the priest Zechariah, being close to the temple where he exercises his priestly functions (according to tradition, at Ain Karem, nine miles to the east of Jerusalem).

This is quite a journey . . . more than eighty miles as the crow flies: almost a week of travel on foot. Was Mary accompanied as would be normal for a young girl? Did she travel alone, as her haste indicates? Luke retains only the essentials of the story, the fervour and the grace of this meeting. The Holy Spirit came upon Mary. He is going to fill Elizabeth. And this is the first prophetic awakening in the New Testament. Two women are its object. They are the first to be baptised in the Spirit (*Luke 1:35* and *41;* cf, *Matthew 3:11; Mark 1:8; Luke 3:16; John 1:33; Acts 1:5; 11, 16*). They are to be the first to prophesy (*Luke 1:42-45* and *46, 55*). For the aged Elizabeth, who is in her sixth month, the visit of Mary, carrying the Son of God made man, is a sudden illumination. Up until that time she had hidden the still secret grace which had put an end to her humiliation as a sterile woman. She gives thanks to God alone:

> The Lord has done this for me, now that it has pleased him to take away the humiliation I suffered in public (*Luke 1:25*).

Now she is 'filled with the Holy Spirit' *(1:41)* at the same time as her son *(1:15)*, she recognises the grace of Mary, greater than her own and praise flows forth from her lips:

> Of all women you are the most blessed, and blessed is the fruit of your womb. Why should I be honoured with a visit from the mother of my Lord? Look, the moment your greeting reached my ears, the child in my womb leapt for joy *(Luke 1:42-44)*.

She confides here her experience as a mother: while the Holy Spirit was filling her, her infant moved within her and she recognised in this the prophetic awakening of this precursor, the last of the prophets, as Elijah had been the first, according to the announcement to Zechariah:

> Even from his mother's womb he will be filled with the Holy Spirit, and he will bring back many of the Israelites to the Lord their God. With the spirit and power of Elijah he will go before him to reconcile fathers to their children and the disobedient to the good sense of the upright, preparing for the Lord a people fit for him (*Luke 1:15-17*).

Elizabeth's expression 'He danced for joy' takes up the Greek word *skirtao* which expresses, in the Bible, the dance of David before the Ark of the Covenant (*2 Samuel 6:16,* according to the Greek translation of Symnacus, *The Truth of Christmas Beyond the Myths*) The expression is not only biblical and poetic, it is exact. Today we can film the foetus in the mother's womb. Early on we see a tiny being with a large head, in a pleasant state of weightlessness, like the cosmonauts, who soon moves happily in a very warm environment. These movements are easier in the first months during which the child is less compressed.

This is certainly a type of dance, a prophetic dance as perceived by Elizabeth, filled by the Holy Spirit: the secret intuition of a mother.

This first page of the gospel is penetrated by a simple and profound theology of two mothers, in deep symbiosis with their infants, still inseparable from them. Elizabeth, filled with the Holy Spirit, understands that her child has also received this grace, within her, for they are both still biologically one single living entity and God unites them in the same grace. This perception explains the apparent anomalies of the account. Mary seems to be on the first plane and Jesus on the second. It is she whom Elizabeth praises first before her Son whom she recognises, however, as Lord:

> Blessed is the fruit of your womb. Why should I be honoured with a visit from the mother of my Lord? (*Luke 1:42-43*).

Why didn't she say: 'May the *Lord* come to me in his mother?' (*The Truth of Christmas Beyond the Myths* p. 145).

These marvellous children remain hidden in their mothers who act alone, speaking and manifesting themselves visibly. There is between the mother and the son a unity of life, an admirable exchange of the divine and the human. In one and the same movement, the Holy Spirit, coming upon Mary, has caused the birth of the Saviour God and consecrated his mother in her new relationship with God. That is why the angel's words allow Mary to stand out in totally stark relief. 'The Holy Spirit will come upon you and the power of the Most High will cover you with its shadow' (*Luke 1:35*). Mary remains an icon of the Incarnation.

Luke's gospel thus transmits an entire theology of the maternal womb and of the Incarnation which Protestant theology of the third world has rediscovered at a time when so many Catholics have lost the concrete meaning of the humanisation of the Son of God.[6]

At the Visitation, Elizabeth praises the faith of Mary to whom God has committed the dawning of the new creation through a new birth:

> Blessed is she who believed that the promise made her by the Lord would be fulfilled.

And here is Mary, glorified by the prophecy of Elizabeth, prophesying in her own turn. But this prophecy is not a response to Elizabeth, a thank you for her very obvious song of praise. Mary renders glory to God alone. This is her Magnificat:

> My soul proclaims the greatness of the Lord and my spirit rejoices in God my Saviour.

As we have established elsewhere,[7] this song goes back to Mary herself.

This is not to say that Mary was a writer, who would have written laboriously at her table as has been alleged by way of ridiculing this hypothesis. She belonged to an oral civilisation in which prayer was transmitted by memory. This canticle of Mary is simply an admirably adapted and updated reminiscence of and throwback to the canticle of Hannah, the mother of Samuel (*1 Samuel 2*).

This canticle, almost 1,000 years prior to Mary's, furnished the revolutionary theme of the Magnificat:

> The bow of the mighty has been broken but those who were tottering are now braced with strength . . .

The inspiration of the Magnificat should not be sought in the Resurrection of Christ even if in fact it may have been transfused with this light after the event. We find some canticles of Resurrection in the epistles of the apostle Paul and they are totally different:

> Wake up, sleeper,
> rise from the dead,
> and Christ will shine on you. (*Ephesians 5:14*).

Mary's inspiration is very far removed from this. She takes up the thousand-year-old canticle of the mother of Samuel:

1 Samuel 2:1-10:
Canticle of Hannah

1 My heart exults in
Yahweh . . .
for I rejoice
in your deliverance . . .
4 The bow of the mighty has
been broken . . .
5 The full fed are hiring themselves out for bread but the
hungry need labour no more . . .
7 Yahweh makes poor and
rich, he humbles and also
exalts . . .
10 he endows his king with
power.

Luke 1:46-55
Magnificat

46 My soul proclaims the
greatness of the Lord (Yahweh)
47 and my spirit rejoices in
God my Saviour
52 He has pulled down princes
from their thrones and raised
high the lowly.
53 He has filled the starving
with good things, sent the rich
away empty.
He has come to the help of
Israel his servant, mindful of his
faithful love.

What Mary refers to in her canticle is not the Resurrection but the meaning of the truly overwhelming events which she had just experienced: the Annunciation and the Visitation. I rejoice in 'God my Saviour'.

She also rejoices in the marvellous grace that God has given to her cousins Elizabeth and Zechariah from whom John the Baptist is to be born. And we have seen how this Semitic text of the canticle alludes to the names of these three people.

Mary, exalted by the message of the angel who has given to her, on the initiative of God, a new name, a name of grace (*1:28*), Mary, become mother of the Son of God, (*1:32* and *35*), invested with his glory (from the Shekinah), as once the Ark of the Covenant had been (*1:35*), gives thanks to God 'for he has done great things for me', she declares in *Luke 1:49.*

Mary is not boastful about this grace but concludes: 'You see before you the Lord's servant' (*1:38*), and gives thanks to God 'Because he has looked upon the humiliation of his servant' *(Luke 1:48).* She insists upon her own singular titles of humility: servant and poor.[8] We are now ready to reread her thanksgiving:

> My soul proclaims the greatness of the Lord and my spirit rejoices in God my Saviour [my Jesus]; because he has looked upon the humiliation of his servant. Yes, from now

on all generations will call me blessed, for the Almighty has done great things for me. Holy is his name. (*Luke 1:46-49*)

Mary extends this personal thanksgiving to all people, of whom she is the personification, the daughter of Zion to whom the prophets announced the fulfilment of the promises: God has exalted her poverty *(1:48).* He likewise lifts up the poor of Israel. This is the expanded theme of the second part *(1:50-54):*

> . . . and his faithful love extends age after age to those who fear him.
> He has used the power of his arm.
> He has routed the arrogant of heart.
> He has pulled down princes from their thrones and raised high the lowly.
> He has filled the starving with good things, sent the rich away empty.

An admirable canticle which the Church sings each day at Vespers. Undoubtedly, it has been so well retained and preserved because it was already being sung in the primitive community of Jerusalem to which Mary belonged and in which she participated.

This second part of the canticle is astonishing, revolutionary in the etymological sense of the word, for it proclaims a reversal of the hierarchies of this world:

— The boastful and the humiliated (v. *51*)
— The powerful and the poor (v. *55*)
— The gluttons and the hungry (v. *53*).

Charles Maurras understood this quite well. In 1913, he praised the Church for having neutralised the 'venom' of this canticle: he demolished Marc Sangnier and the 'democratic priests' who unfolded its liberating power well before any theologies of liberation.[9]

But watch out! It is the revolution of God and not of men that is at stake: a revolution that was sung a thousand years before Mary as we have seen in the case of the canticle of Hannah quoted above. This canticle does not announce vengeance or the reduction of the oppressors to the condition of the oppressed as so many revolutions tend to do, but rather the investiture of the rich with the dignity of the poor.

Mary is not a poor woman transformed into a queen of this world in the manner of Cinderella and fairy tales. She is a queen in the sight of God for all eternity, in her very poverty, through which God exalts her. Her human poverty remains and will be that of her Son: he will be servant and poor as she is servant and poor.

The expressions used by Mary are no less bold: 'He has thrown down the mighty from their thrones', she says. The power on the throne is King Herod, still the triumphant murderer (not for long) who will soon threaten the life of Jesus (*Matthew 2,* cf. *Luke 1:4*). What is surprising is that Mary speaks in the past tense (the Greek *aorist*): 'God has thrown down the mighty from their thrones'. How can he do this? Herod is ever on his throne and the poor are always hungry!

This futuristic past is the anticipated affirmation of the triumph of God. In him the future is as assured as the past. Hope is not deceived by focusing on God who has already won. After having expanded the perspective to the entire people of Israel and to its future, Mary gives thanks for the past, going all the way back to Abraham, the father of believers:

> He has come to the help of Israel his servant,
> mindful of his faithful love
> — according to the promise he made to our ancestors —
> of his mercy to Abraham and to his descendants for ever (*Luke 1:53-55*).

The canticle finishes as it began: it moves from Mary, the final personification of the faith of Israel, to the patriarch Abraham who is its original personification. The Magnificat links them in one act of thanksgiving: it is Mary who expresses it in the name of Abraham and all the generations between him and her.

The episode finishes with the departure of the visitor: Mary will remain with her (Elizabeth) for three months and will return to her home (*1:56*).

The three months are in addition to the six months of Elizabeth's pregnancy, mentioned in *Luke 1:24,26,36*. Did Mary leave Elizabeth sometime before or sometime after the birth of John the Baptist? It would seem to have been sometime after. For the homogeneity of the account, Luke finishes it prematurely with Mary, as he will do, two chapters later, with John the

Baptist: he recounts his imprisonment and his death (*Luke 3:19-20*) before his account of Jesus' baptism (*3:21-22*) in which he is curiously silent about John the Baptist. Likewise for Mary in *1:57-80*.

A further indication along the same line — to the six plus three months are added about eight days for the long journey on foot from Nazareth to the outskirts of Jerusalem, which leads us to believe that Mary remained with Elizabeth until the time of the circumcision of John the Baptist which the gospel, by way of conclusion, recounts (*Luke 1:57-80*). She would thus have been a witness to the canticle of Zechariah, the first part of which is an echo of her Magnificat. It is a thanksgiving for salvation in Jesus the Saviour (*1:69*) which goes back to Abraham and to the Covenant, evoked with reference to the meaning of the name of Zechariah, Elizabeth and John.

Return to Nazareth

What took place upon her return? Undoubtedly we need to speak at this point of Joseph's decision based on his conscience. Popular accounts have disfigured this by dramatising it. This has been done since the fourth or the fifth century. They have invented the *suspicion* of Joseph which is totally foreign to the gospel. In an altogether different way Matthew presents the case of Joseph's conscience. He mentions it in very abrupt terms, which translations have embellished, made more explicit or transposed: Mary had been engaged to Joseph, but before they lived together, she was found to have in her womb the one who was coming from the Holy Spirit.

Joseph's problem is therefore not the brutal fact that Mary was pregnant by someone who was unknown to him. The problem is that the Holy Spirit had brought about this mysterious pregnancy, so mysterious that the text becomes elliptical and does not explain it. We have to explain the phrase in parenthesis in order to render it intelligible. Translations have more or less found a way out by means of circumlocution. Joseph's reflection goes in the same direction: 'Being an upright man, he did not wish to defame her publicly, but resolved to put her away secretly.'

It is because he is upright that Joseph does not wish to defame her. If he judged her guilty, justice would demand that he denounce her. The non-denunciation would not be a matter of justice but of his love, of his pity, of his goodness of heart and soul. The motive of justice runs as follows: I do not have the right to take this woman upon whom God (the Holy Spirit) has placed his hand, or to usurp this mysterious and glorious posterity which is not mine.

Joseph receives his mission as an adoptive father in terms which ordinarily have been poorly translated (the result of not seizing upon the play on words in the Greek particles (*Gar* ...even though... because) which was proposed by X. Leon-Dufour and A. Pelletier in *Recherches de Sciences Réligieuses* 54, 1966, *p* 67-68).

> Joseph son of David, do not be afraid to take Mary home as your wife, because she has conceived what is in her by the Holy Spirit. She will give birth to a son and you must name him Jesus, because he is the one who is to save his people from their sins (*Matthew 1:20-21*).

We do not know anything further about what could have been the dialogue or the tacit understanding of Joseph and Mary, enlightened from within, nor what Mary could have said to Joseph regarding her plan, inspired by God, to remain a virgin. We know nothing about the style of life of this singular household except what we know of other households where the privation of carnal intercourse did not lessen their love and tenderness which, on the contrary, grew ever deeper.

These extraordinary circumstances are motivated by very different reasons: separation by exile; health; irregular marriage, such as spouses who are divorced and remarried and continue to live together as brother and sister. Sometimes also there are the demands of an exceptional mission. For some it is a question of a mystical choice. Such was the case with Jacques and Raissa Maritain after their conversion. Such is the case today with Jean-Baptiste and Nicole Echivard, founders of a community in which all of the members take the vow of chastity. They did so themselves after having had three children. This is not a rational choice. 'We understood that God expected this of us and that it would be a mistake not to do it', they respond when they are asked about it.

So successful are they in preserving their particular secret that they appear as models of complete harmony so that their friends frequently say to them: 'You are definitely a couple who have a very successful marriage.'

This makes them smile since it is true but not exactly on the level on which their friends understand it.

We will return later to the universal values of this white marriage of the Holy Family, and of Jesus' adoption by Joseph, which is not a reduced paternity. We will take special note, on the theological level (chapter 3), of why the virginal conception was necessary from the point of view of God: it is a matter of realising and of signifying, not the creation of a new human person, by the love of a man and a woman, but of another marvellous, singular and unique form of creation: the coming of the pre-existent Son of God among men. The Protestant Karl Barth, reflecting upon these two experiences, very boldly stated that human *eros* would not be the adequate sign of the Incarnation and of divine *agape*.

Christmas at Bethlehem

The first known event after the visit of Mary to Elizabeth is the birth at Bethlehem.

Joseph went to Bethlehem for the census decreed by the Emperor Augustus. An obscure descendant of David, he had to register in the city of birth of his ancestor, the shepherd who had become King of Israel. If it was just a matter pertaining to Joseph why did he choose to bring Mary? Perhaps this was one of the ways that he chose to safeguard the secret of this extraordinary birth. The birth of Jesus followed very closely upon the cohabitation, which took place more than three months after Mary's return from visiting Elizabeth. It would have been important to remove her from the stares of the gossips of Nazareth. Nevertheless, this premature pregnancy seems to have been noticed. The gospel preserves two allusions to it. Firstly the ironic reflection of the people of Nazareth about Jesus who has become a prophet: 'Isn't he the Son of Mary? (this son about whom we know nothing regarding his father!)'

Matthew erases this particular statement and restores the expression which would have been normal: 'Isn't this the son of Joseph?'

Secondly, the allusion is more transparent when Jesus accuses his adversaries of not being true sons of Abraham. They respond to him: 'We were not born illegitimate' (*John 8:41*).

But here again, the bare bones account of the gospels does not satisfy our curiosity nor does it answer our questions regarding the psychology of various people.

Luke does not recount this journey. He mentions it in rather laconic terms solely to show that Jesus was born where David, the young shepherd of Bethlehem who had become king and who received the promise of the Messiah (*2 Samuel 7:14*), was born. This topographical bond between Jesus and David must have appeared much more important to Luke, but this Davidic descent of Jesus through Joseph is obscured and thus minimised by the virginal conception.

Everyone went to register, each to his own town. And so Joseph went from the town of Nazareth in Galilee to Judaea, to David's town of Bethlehem — because he was of the house and lineage of David — to register with Mary, his espoused wife who was with child.

At this time, Joseph takes Mary to his home, and we learn this from *Matthew 1:24*, but Luke continues to refer to this by the word *emnesteumene* (often translated by 'fiancée') which signifies the first level of marriage (before cohabitation), as in *Luke 1:27*. He undoubtedly does this in order to recall that Mary is a virgin.

What do we know about this birth? From the time of the apocryphal books, it has been embroidered with all sorts of legends and tales. Matthew does not tell us anything about it. Luke recounts it with strikingly clear and solemn brevity. He placed it at night (*Luke 2:6-8*):

> . . . while they were there, the time came for her to have her child, and she gave birth to a son, her first-born. She wrapped him in swaddling clothes and laid him in a manger, because there was no room for them in the living space.

Do we need to translate inn as 'living space' or 'shelter for travellers'? This is not certain. We can also translate it as 'traveller's hall'. The same word *katalyma* designates the room of the Last Supper in *Mark 4:14* and *Luke 22:11*. But the difference in translation does not change the meaning. Mary is at the point of giving birth. There is no place for her in the shelter or in the common room in the reception house. They find a manger and its crib, which seems to indicate a stable.

What about the cave in Bethlehem? The gospel doesn't mention it but a very ancient tradition attests to it. By the second century the manger was already a venerated place of pilgrimage but by the time of St Jerome it had disappeared. The early

Christians were very attentive to the details of the birth of Jesus (*cf* Laurentin, *The Truth of Christmas Beyond the Myths*).

In the clear text of Luke, Mary appears to be totally in control of herself and of her movements. There is no mention of a midwife expressing great wonder as is the case in the apocryphal gospels. Rather it is she herself who wraps the child in swaddling clothes. An ancient and firm tradition concerning which I have gathered hundreds of patristic texts strongly favours the view that Mary gave birth without pain. This is less astonishing in our own day when we frequently speak of giving birth without pain as a real possibility for all women. If Russian doctors have been able to perfect this technique, it is because certain women have discovered, by themselves, how to master the mechanisms of birth: breathing, relaxation, muscular control, and so on. After so many centuries, during which this birth is viewed as a joyous mystery, it is curious that certain well-intentioned theologians of the twentieth century distance themselves from the common tradition by describing the pain suffered by Mary in giving birth to Christ that Christmas Day as some type of 'co-redemptive suffering'. Mary was destined for other sorrows and sufferings: those of another childbirth.

Of course the mother of the Lord gave birth to Christ actively like other women. Christian tradition attests to this in contrast to the fantasies of the apocryphal gospels in which Jesus appears suddenly out of nowhere (the *Protoevangelium of James*) or in which he comes through Mary just as he came through the walls after his Resurrection.

The fathers of the Church knew how to read in Luke's text the glance of Mary upon this child who was at the same time both her infant and her God:

> How will I call you, you who are different from us, who became one of us? Will I call you son? ... O You who begot your mother by a new generation .... I am your mother since I have borne you in my womb... I am your servant and your daughter by blood and water, since you have redeemed me (St Ephraim, Fifth Century, *Homily on the Nativity*, 16, in *Études Mariales*, p. 59).

Even more clearly still, Basil of Seleucia stated in 459:

> When she contemplates this divine infant, overcome I

> imagine by love and by fear, they speak together one-to-one in this fashion:
> What name would be appropriate to find for you, oh my infant?
> Man? But your Conception is divine!
> God? But you assumed a human Incarnation! What will I do for you? Do I nourish you with milk? Or will I honour you as a God? Will I have concern for you as a mother? Or will I adore you as a servant? Will I embrace you as a son? Or will I supplicate you like a God? Will I offer you milk or will I offer you incense? (*Homily on the Theotokos* 4, pp. 85, 448 AB).

What follows is the beautiful reflection employed by a modern atheist in order to describe Mary in his *Mystery of Christmas*, a play written and performed during captivity in a German POW camp in 1940:

> The Virgin is pale, she regards her infant. How may we paint her face? It is a face which expresses an anxious wonderment which has appeared but once on a human countenance. Christ is her child,the flesh of her flesh and the fruit of her womb. She has carried him for nine months and will hold him in her bosom and for a few moments the temptation is so strong that she forgets that he is God. She swings him about in her arms and says: 'My little one'. But in other moments, she remains silent and she thinks: God is there, and she is struck with a religious fright before this speechless God, this awesome infant. All mothers are at times struck and frightened before the squirming fragment of their flesh which is their child and they feel themselves to be in exile before this new life which has been formed with their life and about which they harbour strange thoughts. But no child has been more cruelly and more rapidly torn from its mother for He is God and He exceeds in every respect, whatever she can imagine.
>
> But I think that there are other moments which come quickly and slide by in which she feels, at the same time, that Christ is her son, her own little one, and that He is God. She looks at him and she thinks: This God is my child. This divine flesh is my flesh. He is fashioned from me. He has my eyes and the form of his mouth is the form of my own mouth.

He resembles me. He is God and He resembles me. No woman has ever had, as her lot, to possess God for herself alone, a totally little God whom one can take into one's arms and cuddle with kisses, a God so warm who smiles and breathes, a God whom one can touch and cause to laugh. And it would be in these moments that I would paint Mary, if I were a painter.

The author is none other than Jean Paul Sartre (*Bar Jonah*, Christmas play, written during captivity). He gave me permission to quote from it even before it was published. He places this description of Mary in the mouth of a blind exhibitor of portraits: blind, since he is an atheist. It sometimes happens that the blind cause those with perfect vision to see things which they are incapable of seeing.

The shepherds at the crib

Luke tells us in 2:7-20, that some shepherds were in the area. They camped in the fields of Bethlehem, as the young David once did. These poor people, without any fire to warm them or a place to lay their heads, were the first witnesses of the birth and the first 'evangelists' who announced 'the good news' received from on high.

Today... a Saviour has been born to you; he is Christ the Lord (*Luke 2:11*).

The heavenly message provided them with a sign of this glorious event... but one quite ordinary and quite deceptive:

You will find a baby wrapped in swaddling clothes and lying in a manger (*Luke 2:12*).

The shepherds 'came in haste', with all of the openness and willingness to be at the disposal of others which characterise the poor. They find 'Mary and Joseph, and the baby lying in a manger' (*Luke 2:16*). They were not deceived. They recognised Christ the Lord in the very sign of his poverty.

It is here that Luke, for the first time, mentions the mother of Jesus as the source of this account:

As for Mary, she treasured all these things and pondered them in her heart (*2:19*).

The first blood shed

There is even more silence regarding the Circumcision, which is introduced by the solemn refrain regarding fulfilment:

> *When the eighth day came and the child was to be circumcised,* they gave him the name Jesus, the name the angel had given him before his conception.

Mary is not named but she is there, she who had received the mission: 'You must name him Jesus', that is to say Saviour (*Luke 1:31*). What did she feel during this traditional ceremony with the first shedding of his blood preparing her for Calvary?

At the age of sixteen, Arthur Rimbaud described it in a poem written in Latin verse. In the poem, he imagined the reaction of Mary as she viewed the initial wounding of the young Jesus, a carpenter, on a beautiful morning:

> All of a sudden the saw was broken;
> And without his noticing, the tool wounded his fingers.
> The purple blood stained his white robe.
> A muffled cry came forth from her mouth.
> He looked at his mother,
> And hid his reddened fingers under his shirt.
> He pretended to smile and said to her:
> Good day, Mama!
> She frowned and her face was bathed in tears.
> But the child without any emotion:
> Asked, why are you weeping, Mother, don't you know?
> Because the end of this blade has grazed my fingers?
> The time is coming when it will be only proper for you to weep.

The Lord in the temple and the sword of sorrow

Luke begins the account of the Presentation with the same solemnity, and using the same refrain.

> *And when the day came for them to be purified,* in keeping with the Law of Moses, they took him up to Jerusalem to present him to the Lord — observing what is written in the Law of the Lord: 'every first-born male must be consecrated to the Lord' (*Exodus 13:2,12,15*) — and also to offer in sacrifice, in accordance with what is prescribed in the Law of the Lord, a pair of turtledoves or two young pigeons.

Once again Mary is there but she is not named. Luke erases her 'purification' which the law prescribes for mothers on the fortieth day after giving birth and which for a long time continued on in the Church with the ceremony of churching. Rather curiously, he says '*their* purification' in order to transfer this purification to Jerusalem and to the temple which Jesus enters for the first time (R. Laurentin, *The Truth of Christmas beyond the Myths*, pp. 111-119).

This is Mary's meditation transmitted and retained by Luke. He calls this first coming of Jesus to the temple, in order to be brought back, the 'Presentation' (although this rite is unknown). For the event is that 'the Christ-Lord', Jesus 'Saviour' (*Luke 2:11*) comes to fill the temple. This temple had been empty since the Ark of the Covenant disappeared. The coming of the Son of God fills it once again.

The Holy Spirit forewarns two representatives of the 'little remnant' of the poor of Israel — those who were awaiting the Messiah — about the marvellous event.

Simeon runs to the temple and takes Jesus 'into his arms'. Mary, who is not a possessive mother, immediately hands him over to the old man who recognises in him the Saviour and even the Salvation (an abstract word which is the superlative of the title Saviour revealed to the shepherds). In line with Elizabeth (*Luke 1:42-45*), Mary (*1:46-55*) and Zechariah (*1:68-80*), Simeon, in his turn, prophesied:

> Now, Master, you are letting your servant go in peace [that is to say you allow him to die] as you promised; for my eyes have seen the salvation [Jesus Saviour is also salvation] which you have made ready in the sight of the nations; a light of revelation for the gentiles and glory for your people Israel (*Luke 2:29-32*).

Mary is astonished by these prophetic insights of Simeon, but he also has a number of more sombre prophecies for her:

> Look, he is destined for the fall and for the rise of many in Israel, destined to be a sign that is opposed — and a sword will pierce your soul too — so that the secret thoughts of many may be laid bare (*Luke 2:34-35*).

The shadow of the Passion

The shadow of the Passion then falls upon the joyous mysteries of the infancy. The Saviour — Christ the Lord — will be a sign of contradiction. Mary will undergo an after-shock, a deadly sword will pierce her life when the centurion's lance pierces his heart. She does not yet understand what this sword signifies. Every prophecy, before its fulfilment, is obscure.

A woman of eighty-four is present. She is 'Anna, daughter of Phanuel of the tribe of Asher', widowed after seven years of marriage. As *Luke 2* indicates, she is a prophetess.

> She... never left the temple, serving God night and day with fasting and prayer. She came up just at that moment, and began to praise *God*; and she spoke of *the child* to all who looked forward to the deliverance of Jerusalem (*2:37*).

The original text is ambiguous: 'she praised God and spoke of *him*'. Of whom did she speak?

— God, in the immediate context.
— Jesus, in the concrete context which our translation favours.

This ambiguity testifies to the identification of Jesus with God. Mary bore him in her heart and this profound but still obscure insight passed into the account. This 'anomaly', like those preceding it, is not a result of negligence or clumsiness. It passes on the ultimate meaning of a truly profound meditation.

The flight and the exile

The sword of sorrow announces the battle of the prince of darkness against Jesus. It has already begun and Matthew (*2:1-23*) alone brings it to our attention. Some magi from the east, guided by a star, arrive at Bethlehem. Which star? Some astronomical events, confirmed or improvised, have been used in an attempt to identify it: Halley's Comet, a planet passing close to the earth or an exceptional conjunction of stars. These hypotheses are worthless. A normal star would indeed have been able to guide the magi from the east to the west, in accordance with the earth's normal rotation. But this star actually guides them from Jerusalem to Bethlehem: from the north to the south. As John Chrysostom very correctly stated in the fouth century, this is therefore not a natural and cosmic sign but a mysterious manifestation of the glory of God like those which are found throughout the Old Testament up until the showing of the glory of God to the shepherds coming to the crib (*Luke 2:9*).

The consultation at Jerusalem by the magi who are astrologers (undoubtedly when they lost sight of the star mysteriously guiding them) necessarily proved fatal for Jesus. 'Where is the King of the Jews?' these magi ask King Herod. But he was a very jealous tyrant, insecure on his throne, who had just arranged for the assassination of two of his own sons out of fear that their popularity would make them his rivals. This caused the Emperor Augustus to say: 'It is better to be Herod's pig than his son'. (This was a play on words since in Greek the word *hus* (pig) is formed from the same letters as *huios*, son.)

The massacre of the Holy Innocents, which some have suspected of being an invention, does indeed fit the style of Herod. It has been placed in doubt because history has not preserved its memory. But in terms of the scorecard of Herod, this little massacre is usually passed over unnoticed among so many others. Those massacres which history has preserved show that hundreds of lives, particularly of influential people, had been lost. On the eve of his death, Herod had the circus of Jericho filled to capacity with orders given to massacre those in the circus at the moment of his death so that this particular day would be a day of sorrow and tears and would not result in a tremendous outbreak of joy. This was an order which was not executed. The massacre at Bethlehem concerned only poor infants, those who would be ignored by history. Bethlehem and its environs probably consisted of a great deal fewer than 1,000 inhabitants. The slaughter could have included at most twenty children. We need not interpret the silence of secular history as a denial of events which history had no reason to preserve.

When the magi came to Bethlehem, they found the child in a 'house', according to Matthew. We can take this word in its proper sense, for after the birth, Joseph must have set about finding a house in this city where he had some family.

Matthew finally deals with the flight into Egypt about which we have said nothing and about which a great deal has been embroidered and concocted even to the point of making Jesus into an initiate of Egyptian magi. This journey lasted a short time for Herod died a few months later, possibly some weeks after the birth of Jesus, and so they returned to Galilee (*Matthew 2:13-25*).[10]

The lost child

As for the childhood at Nazareth, Luke furnishes us with a significant episode. Jesus' parents go up each year to Jerusalem, the central place of worship for all devout Jews. The law prescribes their going there three times a year (*Exodus 23:14-17; 34:22-23; Deuteronomy 16:16*). But when someone lived as far away as Nazareth (over 100 kilometres) it was understood that a yearly visit would suffice. And this visit would take place at the feast of Passover. At the age of twelve, Jesus was on the pilgrimage. Was it quite possibly for his bar mitzvah (the equivalent of our confirmation)? This is suggested, but perhaps the custom had not taken hold since this ritual in which a child became a 'son of the law' would usually have taken place at the age of thirteen or fourteen years rather than at the age of twelve. At this age, which is the first step in maturity from childhood and a prefiguration of adulthood, Jesus is going to affirm himself prophetically by a surprising escapade. As they were returning at the end of the feast, the child Jesus remained behind unknown to his parents. Thinking he was in their party, they continued their journey for a day looking for him among their relatives and acquaintances. Not finding him, they returned to Jerusalem in search of him (*Luke 2:43-45*).

This historical datum eliminates the caricatures which have made Mary into a possessive and inseparable mother who never left Jesus on his own. No, she allows him to wander freely within the group on pilgrimage: a large family in which each person depends on everyone else, under the eye of God. It takes Mary a day to perceive that Jesus is not in the caravan.

And this is what came about:

> Three days later, they found him in the Temple, sitting among the teachers, listening to them, and asking them questions; and all those who heard him were astounded at his intelligence and his replies (*Luke 2:46-47*).

Despite an almost solemn tone, the description remains modest. Jesus does not behave as a master among masters but as a child. He questions and responds like a child. The gospel is careful not to attribute to him discussions beyond his age as do the apocryphal gospels. According to the *Syro-Arabic Gospel of the Infancy*, he presents one of the teachers with an explanation about astronomy: 'the number of spheres and heavenly bodies with their nature, their powers, their oppositions, their combinations by three, four and six, their risings and fallings, their position calculated in minutes and seconds and other matters which go beyond the reach of our reason' (*Syro-Arabic Gospel of the Infancy*, ch 50, Peeters Editions, Paris, 1914, 2, p. 62). He responds to a philosopher who is well-versed in medicine, with a dissertation regarding physics, metaphysics, hyperphysics and hypophysics concerning the forces of bodies and their constitution, their nature, their energies and their influence on nerves, bones, veins, the arteries, tendons and on the properties of cold, hot, dry, humid and so on.

In Luke's gospel there is nothing extraordinary or beyond measure. Seeing him, his parents were amazed and his mother said to him:

> My child, why have you done this to us? See how worried your father and I have been, looking for you. (*Luke 2:48*).

The word *odynomenoi*, which we translate by *anxious* is a very shocking and extreme term. In the New Testament, it signifies the anguish of death and the torments of hell. Mary transmitted this term because her sorrow was immense, that of every mother who looks for a lost son fearing that he is dead. At this moment, she had a premonition and first realisation of the sword of sorrow which had been announced by Simeon. God does not give to those who love him (no more than he gave to himself) a bed of roses. He enlists them in his own very difficult trial of the Redemption. When Mary passed on her recollections she knew to what lengths this would lead her.

At this point, she is astonished by this amazing escapade. But Jesus, the 'submissive' child, speaks firmly. He responds with an enigmatic question:

> Why were you looking for me? Did you not know that I must be in my Father's house? (*Luke 2:49*)

But they do not understand what he is saying to them, as Luke indicates, in accordance with the remembrances of Mary (*2:48* and *51*).

It would truly take a long time for them to understand this prophetic deed of the child Jesus. Mary will understand it fully only after the Resurrection. These three days, during which Jesus disappeared, at Jerusalem, during the feast of Passover, prefigured the three days of his death in the tomb and of his return to his Father in order to prepare a place for us, in this same Jerusalem, in another Passover; the true Passover (R. Laurentin, *The Truth of Christmas Beyond the Myths*).

The hidden life

In the meantime, until his public life begins, Jesus remains buried in the history of the poor. What we can discover of this hidden life is his daily labour as a carpenter, instructed first of all by Joseph in the use of the hand tools of the period. For Joseph, then for Jesus alone, it was a matter of the weight of the beams (even then the beams!), and of serving customers.

It appears clear that Joseph died before Jesus began his public life. This is what *Mark 6:3* seems to indicate where he refers to Jesus as 'the carpenter' and not 'the son of the carpenter', as *Matthew 13:55* does. With Mary, will Jesus weep over the death of Joseph, as he would weep over the death of Lazarus? We can suppose this to be the case but the gospel does not say anything about it.

The separation

When Jesus left around the age of thirty, as *Luke 3:23* tells us, he was baptised by John the Baptist, spent forty days in the desert and then began his ministry.

For Mary this was separation and solitude. We are astonished not to find her among the group of women who followed Jesus throughout his ministry as *Luke 8:1-3* reports:

> Mary surnamed the Magdalene, Joanna the wife of Herod's steward Chuza, Susanna, and many others who provided for them out of their own resources.

These women were certainly his disciples throughout the entire period when he was travelling. Such was not Mary's vocation. She had to share in the hidden life of Jesus, not in the works, triumphs and contradictions of his ministry.

Her vocation as mother included the trial of separation and a discreet share in the public career of her son whose preaching, trips, miracles and arrest by his enemies she would learn of only by hearsay.

Where Mary suggests Jesus' first sign

John the Evangelist relates an episode unknown in the synoptics:

Mary suggests to Jesus his 'first sign' at Cana of Galilee and thus brings about the inauguration of his ministry. Here, again, the starkness of the account does not permit us to know the full details or the psychology of the characters in the account.

Mary has been invited to a wedding feast at Cana, not far from Nazareth — the marriage of a family member or friend. Jesus turns up with his disciples.

Marriages are ostentatious occasions for which huge reserves are put away. It is a time of festivity and of generosity. Jesus is invited to the wedding along with his disciples. But there is no longer any wine, for the wine of the wedding feast had run out (*John 2:2*). This is because of the number of guests. Mary says to her son:

> They have no wine (*2:3*).

You can well imagine the feminine eye of Mary, mistress of the house, and her compassion for her host who is faced with this tremendous need. To run out of supplies on the occasion of a wedding was to lose face. The feast and its attendant joy would turn into a fiasco. What does Mary suggest? Is she to intercede? Jesus seems to realise this but dismisses her request:

> Woman, what do you want from me? (literally, 'What is that to you and to me?') My hour has not yet come (*24*).

The response is doubly negative:

1 Jesus calls Mary 'woman' and not 'mother' as was customary, in order to distance himself from her.
2 The Semitic formula: 'what is that to you and to me?' is employed to dismiss a pressing request. The devil used it to command Jesus to depart:

> What is that to you and to me, Jesus of Nazareth? Have you come to destroy us?

Psychoanalysis draws a feminist interpretation from this: Jesus shows the weakness of his masculine psychology. He flees from his awesome duty: he speaks like a 'devil', France Quéré dares to say. It is Mary who upholds the plan of God: stronger in her femininity than Jesus reduced in his virility. Although a Protestant, Quéré dares to up the mariological ante:

> Mary had given birth to Jesus at Christmas. Now (at Cana)

> she gives birth to Christ (France Quéré, *Les Femmes Dans L'Évangile*, Paris, Seuil, 1982, p. 144).

She is echoing, with an added nuance, the commentary of the psychoanalyst, Françoise Dolto:

> It is the strength of Mary which gave birth, and please allow me to use this word, *phallically* to Jesus, by an act of power... Perhaps it was at this precise moment, during the wedding feast of Cana, that Mary became Mother of God (*L'Évangile Au Risque de la Psychanalyse*, Paris, 1977, p. 300).

What is clear in this enigmatic gospel is that Mary is not rebuffed. Despite Jesus' refusal, she remains confident. She has hope — for she says to the servants:

> Do whatever he tells you (*2:4*).

The gospel of Cana gives us the final two statements of Mary who will be silent at the Cross and at Pentecost. These sentences are complementary and significant.

— The first is addressed to Jesus in order to intercede with him;
— The second is addressed to the servants in order to have them turn towards Jesus who will do the rest.

The evangelist seems to have chosen these sentences because they signify Mary's attitude up until that day. She continues to repeat these words to Jesus, faced with the sad plight of the men:

> They have no wine! (no more joy)

And to us:

> Do whatever he tells you.

The evangelist was conscious of the eschatological and universal implications of this scene.

Jesus then intervenes. There are six stone jars each containing two to three measures (a measure being about forty litres, the gospel suggests the wondrous figure of 720 litres) equivalent today to more than two large barrels.

> Jesus said... 'Fill the jars with water.

And they filled them up to the brim.

Then he said to them:

> Draw some out now and take it to the president of the feast (*John 2:7-8*).

The president tastes and is astonished that the bridegroom has kept the good wine to the end (*John 2:10*).

What is important is the conclusion. The first sign has established the faith of the disciples. John sees there a sign of the new Covenant.

> This was the first of Jesus' signs: it was at Cana in Galilee. He revealed his glory, and his disciples believed in him (*John 2:11*).

Is it, as F.M. Braun alleges, after this scene that we have the immediate separation up until the hour of Calvary? This would be to forget the following verse:

> After this, he went down to Capernaum with his mother and his brothers and his disciples, but they stayed there only a few days (*John 2:12*).[11]

The public life

This time it is the separation up until the hour when Jesus aranges a meeting with Mary: the hour of Calvary, the hour of Redemption (*John 2:4* and *19:27*).

Mary returns to her home, doubly empty as a result of her widowhood and the departure of Jesus. She experiences the trial of many women, and learns to live more deeply still in the service of God and the love of others, putting up with the tongue-in-cheek comments about Jesus in his own family, 'for his brothers did not believe in him', as *John 7:5* reports.

During the three years of Jesus' ministry, there would only be rare encounters. There is the intrigue of the clan to bring Jesus to Nazareth. Mary would be called upon to play her part by those in charge (*Mark 3:20, 31-35; Matthew 12:46-50; Luke 8:19-21*).

She saw Jesus then on his rare visits to Nazareth. The accounts of the synoptics seem to indicate three such occasions which Luke combines into one — *Luke 4:15-22* — which corresponds to the historical context of *Matthew 4:13*, in which Jesus seems well received:

— *Luke 4:23-24* which corresponds to *Matthew 13:53-58* and

Mark 6:1-6, where Jesus, who was not properly received, performs no miracle.
— *Luke 4:25-30*, the cnd of the Galilean ministry.

But what place did Mary play in these encounters? We have no idea.

Compassion

And now let us look at Mary setting out for the Passover feast of April in the year 30 AD, the Passover of the sword of sorrows. She does not know it. Was she present at the Last Supper — on the eve of Jesus' arrest? The gospel only mentions the disciples as being there. It is not specific: 'the twelve'. The group could be larger. It could include the women disciples who follow Jesus (*Luke 9:-3*). There is nothing to say that they had been excluded. And what would they have done? The Passover was a family meal. Mary normally took part in it. Even though the gospel is silent about this, the likelihood that she was present is still strong.

How did Mary learn of Jesus' trial? We do not know and the synoptics do not mention her presence at Golgotha. But John the Evangelist, 'the disciple whom Jesus loved', the exemplary disciple who was entrusted to his mother, testifies to this presence. Here as elsewhere, the objections of R. Bultmann, generally repeated by Catholic exegetes, form part of a system of demythology and suspicion which has scarcely any more value then the suspicions of King Lear regarding the fidelity of his wife. If John the Evangelist is symbolic, he is a faithful witness of the reality in which he knows how to discern what is essential. He is, along with Mark, the most realistic and the most concrete of the evangelists. In history, as in human relations, it is a good rule never to place a testimony in doubt if you do not have serious enough reasons for doing so. And it is thus that history is practised except when it is a matter of the Bible, where doubts are positively obligatory! Here again, the gospel does not satisfy our curiosity. It does not specify the psychology or the sentiments of those involved. It reports, with brevity and extreme compactness, Jesus' final testament. Let us unfold all of it right now.

Jesus had lost everything, including his friends and his disciples, who had fled. Everything had been taken away from him: his freedom, his clothing for which the soldiers cast lots.

His life was about to be taken from him. He gives away everything which he still possesses: first of all his mother, present at the foot of the Cross. This account expresses a sorrowful and generous transfer, which the play on possessive adjectives in some versions demonstrates strikingly. Mary, the mother of Jesus, is first of all called *his* mother (twice), then *the* mother with the article, without the possessive, as if her motherhood were without object, in order to end up with the word of transfer addressed to John (and to us through him): this is *your mother*.

> Near the Cross of Jesus stood his mother and his mother's sister, Mary the wife of Clopas and Mary of Magdala.
> Seeing his ['the'] mother and the disciple whom he loved standing near her, Jesus said to his ['the'] mother,
> 'Woman, this is your son!'
> Then to the disciple he said,
> 'This is your mother.'
> And from that hour, the disciple took her into his home.

First of all, it is John who is entrusted to Mary: 'Behold your son'. The beneficiaries of this transfer are John and each one of us.

Mary is entrusted to John and he takes her into his home. Jesus inaugurates a reciprocity of love and assistance between mother and son. It is up to us to understand it. The text does not express the drama of Mary. What a horrible torture for a mother to see her son spat upon, condemned to death, prepared for execution, scourged, all bloody, nailed to the wood of the Cross, his mouth contorted from the lock-jaw suffered by the crucified, to which Doctor Barbet attests. So atrocious and deadly is this tortue that it is impossible for one to be able to tolerate it or even inflict it for a sustained period of time.

Why did God allow this? He had spared his adoptive father this suffering. Shouldn't he also have spared his mother?

But Jesus, who did not spare himself anything and who shared everything with his mother wanted also to share this with her. It was her compassion: her giving birth in sorrow to new sons, her sinful sons whom she received in place of the best of sons, humanly destroyed, by this death. Such is the mystery beyond all psychology, a mystery of love without limit. Mary to whom the Saviour-mystery of birth had been entrusted also shares in the mystery of death.

The final appearance

After that, is there silence regarding Mary? Not altogether, for we find her again among the disciples assembled in the upper room in Jerusalem (perhaps the very room in which the Last Supper took place), in order to await *the one* whom Jesus had promised: the Holy Spirit who is going to establish the Church and transform the fearful apostles into witnesses and martyrs.

Did the risen Christ appear to Mary, his mother? The gospel says nothing about this. Since the fourth century several fathers of the Church, including Ephrem and Chrysostom, thought so. Yet this was so because Mary Magdalene was confused with Mary, the mother of Jesus.

Even though Jesus did not grant Mary the privilege of the first appearance it is clear that she was present at the last. Before departing, Jesus renewed his promise:

> The Holy Spirit (which) will come on you ...
> As he said this he was lifted up while they looked on, and a cloud took him from their sight ... So, from the Mount of Olives they went back to Jerusalem, a short distance away, no more than a Sabbath walk; and when they reached the city, they went to the upper room where they were staying; there were Peter and John, James and Andrew, Philip and Thomas, Bartholomew and Matthew, James, sonof Alphaeus, Simon the Zealot, and Jude son of James. With one heart all these joined constantly in prayer, together with some women, including *Mary the mother of Jesus*, and with his brothers (*Acts 1:9-14*).

Mary is certainly among this group which, returning from the final appearance, goes up once more to the upper room in Jerusalem, and sets about the task of being fervent in prayer in order to prepare for the coming of the Holy Spirit. She is the only person, apart from the apostles, mentioned by name. She is placed, as it were, as a hinge between the two groups:

— the disciples who had accompanied Jesus in his ministry;
— his family.

She belongs to both of them: women and family.

After having seen Jesus for the last time on earth, this now becomes for Mary a fourth trial of separation: after the loss of Jesus at the age of twelve years, his departure for his public life, and his death, this is the ultimate absence which leaves her in the night of faith and of the senses. It is in this austere condition that she prays.

The coming of the Holy Spirit

For forty days Mary was at the very pinnacle of the prayer of the Church. The splendour of her faith was, for this community in the process of being born, the greatest good, as they waited for the coming of the Holy Spirit and the celebration of the Holy Eucharist which seems only to have begun after Pentecost (*Acts 2:46*). This ardent flame of Mary attracts the fire of the Holy Spirit. Thus that foundational event comes to pass with Mary at the very forefront.

> When Pentecost Day came round, they had all met together, when suddenly there came from heaven a sound as of a violent wind which filled the entire house in which they were sitting; and there appeared to them tongues as of fire; these separated and came to rest on the head of each of them. They were all filled with the Holy Spirit and began to speak different languages as the Spirit gave them power to express themselves (*Acts 2:1-4*).

What is taking place is the 'baptism in the Spirit', announced by Jesus before his departure.

> John baptised with water but, not many days from now, you are going to be baptised with the Holy Spirit (*Acts 1:5*).

Mary is included (by name) in the group of 120 disciples (*Acts 1:14-15*) of which it is said: 'All ... began to speak different languages as the Spirit gave them power to express themselves' (*Acts 2:4*). The glossolalia (or speaking in tongues) was undoubtedly this community experience with which other groups have experimented since then: the inspired humming of a musical prayer. This harmony which attracts the crowd was (musically) understood by all and contributed to convincing them of the interior event which was going to transform the world.

The final years

After that, the evangelists are silent. Did Mary accompany John to Ephesus according to the rather impressive visions of Katharina Emmerich? History cannot be based on these visions.

All of the cross-references and cross-checkings which she attempts to gather together are, in spite of everything, quite weak, slender and of little weight.

The tomb at Gethsemane

There would have been a great deal more likelihood of Mary's tomb being in Jerusalem. The monument discovered at Gethsemane corresponds to the earliest apocryphal descriptions regarding her death, which Father Bagatti, the archaeologist who discovered her tomb, stresses. But the apocryphal stories regarding the death and the Assumption, like those of the infancy, are too gratuitous, fantastic and divergent to be dependable. If some nuggets of real value remain among the quite impure collection of minerals we have not as yet found any means of identifying them.

Beyond history

Chapter 12 of Revelation evokes Mary's destiny beyond history. This vision projects into the heavens and towards the future what the Gospel of John tells us of Mary, mother of Jesus (*John 2:1* and *19:25*) and mother of the disciples (*19:27*). The woman of Revelation verifies both of these traits: mother of the Messiah (*Revelation 12:2-5*), she also has other children: the disciples (*12:17*). As in the gospel (*John 2:4* and *19:26*), this mother receives the name of *woman* (*12:4,6*), in reference to Eve, according to *Genesis 3*, repeated in *Revelation 12:9*. Like Luke and John, the author of Revelation sees in the mother of Christ the daughter of Zion, the personification of the new people, the personification of the Church. And like Luke, he seems to identify her with the Ark of the Covenant (the dwelling place of God). He juxtaposes them in two successive verses (*11:19* and *12:1*):

> Then the sanctuary of God in heaven opened, and the ark of the covenant could be seen inside it. Then came flashes of lightning, peals of thunder and an earthquake and violent hail. Now a great sign appeared in heaven: a woman, robed with the sun, standing on the moon, and on her head a crown of twelve stars. She was pregnant, and in labour, crying aloud in the pangs of childbirth. Then a second sign appeared in the sky: there was a huge red dragon with seven heads and ten horns, and each of the seven heads crowned with a

> coronet. Its tail swept a third of the stars from the sky and hurled them to the ground, and the dragon stopped in front of the woman as she was at the point of giving birth, so that he could eat the child as soon as it was born. The woman was delivered of a boy, the son who was to rule all the nations with an iron sceptre, and the child was taken straight up to God and to his throne, while the woman escaped into the desert, where God had prepared a place for her to be looked after for twelve hundred and sixty days (*Revelation 11:19-12:6*).

At the end of the chapter, the dragon, who was powerless against the woman, went away to make war '*on the rest of her children,* who obey God's commandments and have in themselves the witness of Jesus'. (*Revelation 12:17*).

These children are disciples, whom Jesus entrusted to Mary, in accordance with what we read in *John 19:25-27*.

The Apocalypse seems to announce the visits of the mother of Christ throughout the course of history. The woman clothed with the 'sun of Justice' (namely Christ) spends her heaven doing good on earth. She loves to visit the Church as she visited her cousin Elizabeth (*Luke 1:39-56*) and her friends at Cana (*John 12:1*). The great apparitions which have marked the Church of modern times shed light upon the Book of Revelation.

— Those of Guadalupe (Mexico 1531) established, in an Indian context, the new Church of the New World and this foundational role is being recognised more and more.
— The apparitions at Lourdes have reawakened the important place of the poor at a time when Thier's motto was: 'Enrich yourselves'. They restored hope in God and the importance of miracles at the precise time when rationalism was at the height of its influence.
— Fatima launched, once more, the same message with a new dimension in the history of salvation, at a time of crisis in the history of the world.

These and other apparitions have rekindled faith even up to our own day.

This is not the place to judge the apparitions or to present a history of them.[12] But frequently the description found in Revelation can be recognised in them: the woman clothed with the sun, enveloped in a light which precedes her and engulfs her. At Guadalupe and elsewhere she had the moon under her feet, and often a crown of twelve stars. And she is present much more continuously, discreetly and efficaciously in the daily life of the Church and in each of us.

Reference to the Apocalypse takes us beyond history, into the mystical domain of vision and the future.

Return to history

To conclude, let us return to history. We have stressed the laconic and sporadic character of our knowledge of Mary. A complete or coherent life cannot be written about her. But scripture allows us to have faith in a number of data such as: her name, her village, her marriage, some of her journeys and soon, some luminous insights which manifest her dynamic and profound connections with Christ and the Church in accordance with her vocation. Instead of making up stories, we have focused instead on this essential collection of data.

Mary and time

One of the greatest facts which emerges from all this is that this woman is situated at the critical hinge of time: before Christ, with Christ throughout his life and after Christ. From an even more penetrating perspective, she belongs to all the ages of salvation: new Eve, the point of departure for the new creation. According to the gospels, she is linked to the period prior to the fall: 'younger than sin'. She concludes the Old Testament, she introduces the Son of God into the world, precedes the Church, and is on hand for Christ's birth, death and Resurrection: an eschatological icon of the Church.

Her place in the structure of the gospels

The brief mentions of Mary in the gospels come together beautifully in order to allow us to become aware of what is essential.

— *Luke 1-2* and *Matthew 1-2*, referred to by the apostle Paul in *Galatians 4:4*, show Mary at the beginning of Jesus' life and during his hidden life.
— John helps us to become aware of her effective role at the beginning and the end of the public life of Christ. Cana and Calvary are similar in their particular reference to 'the hour

of Jesus', and these episodes play a key role in his gospel, which, in its very structure, gives a role to women. Each of the three books of his gospel, the Book of Signs, the Book of the Passion, the Book of the Resurrection, begins with two episodes involving women in which they play a role of faith and anticipation:

1 Mary (*John 2:1-12*) and the Samaritan Woman (*4:7-42*) who, in the Book of Signs, evangelises this marginal people.
2 The sisters of Lazarus who, in the Book of the Passion, introduce the signs of his burial (*12:1-7*) and Resurrection (*11:21-44*).
3 Mary Magdalene, in the Book of Resurrection (*John 20*), was the first visitor to the tomb, privileged to behold the first apparition.

Mary opens the Book of Signs and holds a central place in the Book of the Passion (*John 19:25-27*). In this, she is not in opposition to the rest of women (as a certain brand of Christian feminism has alleged), but she illustrates, along with others, the prophetic and anticipatory role of women in the work of salvation. There is something specific in her role. Unlike other women (the Samaritan, the sisters of Lazarus, Mary Magdalene), she is characterised as 'mother': 'mother of Jesus' (*2:1; 19:25*); 'mother of the disciples' (*19:26-27*). And that gives her a particularly unprecedented place.

Mary and the Holy Spirit

If we ask ourselves about the meaning of Mary according to this gospel history, one of the constants that we observe is that Mary appears linked to the Holy Spirit. Everything begins with him:

> The Holy Spirit will come upon you (*Luke 1:35*).

And she is there, once more, when the promise of Jesus to his apostles is fulfilled:

> The Holy Spirit will come on you (*Acts 1:8*).

Everything that Luke says is understood between these two references to the Holy Spirit: the Protopentecost of the Annunciation and Pentecost (*Acts 1:14-2; 1-12*).

According to John's symbolism, the two episodes in which John places Mary — Cana (*2:1-12*) and Calvary (*19:25-27*) — are also Pentecosts.

— Cana is presented with constant reference to Pentecost, the feast of the covenant, as a new Pentecost, a new covenant, which establishes the faith of the apostles. See Exodus 19 and the Targums.[13]

— At Calvary (*John 19*), Jesus gives away his mother, who is standing beneath him as he 'gave up his spirit' (*John 19:30*), at his very death: the new covenant is sealed in the Spirit, water and blood (*19:35*).

This deep and intimate bond with Jesus and his work, found in the gospel, illustrates what remains to be said about Mary's place in dogma. In the gospel, Mary appears as a free, dynamic woman who is anticipating salvation, full of creativity, and in no way in opposition to other women but rather like them. She is totally related to Christ, totally related to the Holy Spirit, that is to say totally related to God, in a two-fold dynamic of service and of thanksgiving. The story of the gospels, which is a history of salvation, introduces us to dogma.

Notes

1 René Laurentin, *Marie, signe de contradiction au XVIIe siècle*, to be published in les *Actes du Congrès de Malte*, Rome, Academia Mariana, via Merulana 124.

2 Don Pasquale Silla, *Per il bimillenario della nascita di Maria* in *L'Osservatore Romano*, 31 August 1983, *p* 4.

3 *Maria nell' Avvento del Duemila* in *L'Osservatore Romano*, 30 September 1983, p. 1: an article in which some have thought they recognised the pen of Father Spiozzi.

4 In the Bible, we find frequent examples of parents marrying off their children without consulting them (Genesis 29:15-20; 1 Samuel 18:20-26, 25:40); and yet we also find children exercising their freedom of choice (Genesis 29:18-20; 1 Samuel 18:20-26; 25:40), even against the will of the parents (Genesis 26:34; Judges 14:1-10).

5 The very remote possibility that Jesus was an illegitimate son of Mary need not be dismissed out of hand... that Jesus was illegitimate does not contradict Christian love, etc, X. Pikaza, *Los Origines de Jesus*, Salamanca, 1976, p. 32.

6 Choan-Seng Song, Third Eye Theology, Maryknoll, Orbis Books, 1979, ch. 6, pp. 124-140.

7 R. Laurentin, *The Truth of Christmas beyond the Myths*, St Bede's Press, Petersham, Massachusetts, 1986.

8 Just like Elizabeth, Mary thanks God for having regarded her in her poverty, because of her poverty.

9 Charles Maurras, *De l'Action Francaise et la religion catholique*, 1913, re-edited under the title *Évangile et democratie* in *Le Chemin de Paradis*, Paris, Bo-card, 1920, p. 260-264. The theme is treated in a polemical fashion in *Democratie*, 3 August 1913: The democratic priests did not compose the Magnificat: We forget that the Church sings it in ways which do not allow for an evil notion being derived from it, except in the deliberately corrupted minds exemplified by Marc Sangier and Emile Olivier.

10 Note that the very stylised gospels only rarely note significant facts. Matthew runs up against an impasse with the Annunciation and Luke with the flight into Egypt. Thus he mentions the return to Nazareth after the Presentation.

> They went back to Galilee, to their own town of Nazareth.
> And as the child grew to maturity, he was filled with wisdom, and God's favour was with him.

11 F.M. Braun who wrote a beautiful book on Mary in the gospel of John was so focused upon and even befuddled by this idea that his book, devoted to the sixteen verses of John on Mary, omits John 2:12 regarding the trip to Capernaum.

12 René Laurentin, *Pelerinages, Sanctuaires, Apparitions*, Paris, OEIL, 1983.

13 A. Serra, *Contributi dell'antica letteratura guidaica per l'esegesi di GV 2, 1-12 e 19, 25-27*, Rome, Marianum, 1977.

14 R. Laurentin, *Sens et historicité de la Conception virginale in Mélanges C. Balic*, Roma, 1971, pp. 515-542.

15 S. Benko, *Protestants, Catholics and Mary*, Valley Forge, Judson Press, 1968, pp. 129-144.

3

MARY IN DOGMA

Mary has an inescapable place in theology, for theology (a Greek word which signifies knowledge of God, *theos*) is not knowledge of God *in himself* but of God the *Saviour*. And Mary illustrates, better than any other human person, the salvific plan of God. She was the very point of departure for this plan: she formed Christ, she committed herself unconditionally, as servant of the Lord (*Luke 1:38; cf. 1:45*), before every other creator and better than any other. Thus, by her union with Christ she is the prototype of the Church and of every Christian.

By her union with Christ she has a vital place in Christian dogma. Because of her unique and specific bonds with Christ, she is a pivotal point in Christian anthropology.

Dogma and love

Dogma, from the Greek word *dogma*, meaning prescription, signifies what we must believe: what we must not fail to recognise in order to recognise God, and therefore to love him. Nothing is more important than to know God and to experience this relationship of love, which is both discreet and immeasurable, and which he wishes to establish with us. This love is folly: folly of the Cross, but, first of all, the folly of Mary's pregnancy and the birth of the Son of God. It is folly on the part of the creator for having chosen a creature to be his mother: not a 'surrogate mother' as is stupidly said but a real, untransferable mother. God loved this mother madly, as he has loved us, even to the point of death. This far surpasses our love. Let us accept being surpassed, as otherwise we would no longer be Christians. Theology which reduces God to our human perspective is no longer theology but the burial of theology, the obsequies of the death of God.

Theology is the understanding of the saving love of God. This is why anyone who denies dogma destroys the possibilities of authentic love and destroys himself since man, without God, falls apart. The prescriptions of dogma bind us, not under penalty of external sanctions but under the penalty of alienation from God, who is our final destiny.

Salvation in Jesus Christ begins concretely, historically, through this woman from whom he asked the free consent to become man among men. And as we have seen, she has remained present to him from his birth to his death and, even now, in eternal glory.

God has revealed Jesus Christ to us by the crib, by the Cross, by the empty tomb: signs of his poverty, of his love, of his Resurrection. He has also revealed himself to us, in a more vital and personal manner, through Mary his mother, for the Mother of God is not any particular type of mother. God who could not end up in the corruption of the tomb, as is the case in any death, could not come into this mother without transfiguring her person and her maternity, transfiguring her without disfiguring her. The Mother of God is not like the mother hen employed to hatch duck eggs whose aquatic nature, being foreign to her nature, upsets the brooding mother hen on the lakeside. Mary has not made a demi-God or a superman of the Son of God but, rather, a real man, even though he is assumed by God. She is recognised in this son and he is recognised in this mother. In her, the *Verbum*, eternal image of the invisible God, has become a temporal and visible image.

Three dogmatic layers

Whence flow the Christian dogmas which concern, in varying degrees, the Blessed Virgin Mary?

Later on we will examine:

1 Since the Son of God is born of her, she is Mother of God in person. The Fathers insist that this unique motherhood calls for virginity as its specific sign. It also calls for holiness. In accordance with the profound logic of God, these three points of dogma form only one layer. This first dogmatic galaxy is biblical and the Church, from the earliest centuries, before the middle of the fifth century, was more explicitly conscious of it. Let us begin with this primary and fundamental source of revelation.

2 The two dogmas defined during this modern era, regarding Mary's immaculate beginning and her glorious end.

3 Two more fundamental dogmatic facts which have not been formally defined: her place in the work of salvation and in Christian worship.

1. BIBLICAL DOGMAS: MOTHER OF GOD, VIRGIN, HOLY

A. Mother of God

Mary had been chosen by God so that he could become man among men. This is her *raison d'être* in the plan of salvation. By conceiving, forming, bearing and raising this child who is God, she became Mother of God. This is the central and fundamental point concerning Mary.

A biblical and traditional language

This is certainly well attested to in the Scriptures, in which Christ is Lord, and Mary is his mother. She is formally Mother of God according to *Luke 1:43*, in which the word 'Lord' is to be taken in its strictest sense.

What increases the difficulty is that the Church first expressed this dogma by a paradoxical and vulnerable expression: *theotokos*. This Greek word literally signifies: the one who gives birth to God, *theo*. The suffix *tokos*, which is used to form more than a hundred Greek words, was familiar to doctors and biologists. It is the equivalent of our suffix 'par', in viviparity, oviparity, primiparity (this last word being used by doctors to designate a woman who is giving birth for the first time). *Theo-tokos*, paradoxically, at one and the same time connotes the fact that there is something more divine and something more animal in the Incarnation: God and giving birth, coming into the world through her in a more concrete, fleshly and violent fashion. This was repugnant to the Greeks since God was unchangeable, incorruptible, impassible. The implication that God was born seemed to be a disintegration and a blasphemy.

That is why the Patriarch Nestorius, a prelate, who was renowned for his wisdom and his balance, criticised the term *theotokos*. He had much more reason for doing so since this title, which had come from Egypt, was originally used to designate the goddess Isis: *manu-ti*, a word which had the same structure and the same meaning as *theotokos*. But the meaning had been corrected perfectly.

Cyril of Alexandria then reacted. He defended the Egyptian title while, at the same time, attacking the Patriarch who was running the risk of splitting the unity of Christ.

The Council of Ephesus (431) was the defender not of Mary,

but of this unity. It was absolutely necessary to confirm that God became man in person. It is therefore he indeed who was born, who has suffered, who has died, in person, according to his humanity. This grammatical attribution to the Son of God of what he had lived out in his humanity was known as *communication of idioms*: namely the attribution to his person of everything that he experienced in his own human life.

The paradox which can appear shocking in the expression *theotokos* is very simply inherited from the Prologue of St John, 'The Word was made flesh'. This bold formula of *John 1:14* is paradoxical. Like *theotokos*, it links together both extremes: the divine and the fleshly.

The formula is incomplete since it would be better to say 'the Word became man'. Christ had not simply assumed flesh. He had assumed a complete *humanity*: body and soul (intelligence, will, human freedom). He is fully man, at the same time being fully God: perfect man and perfect God, as the Fathers say. The Latins preferred a less shocking but more abstract expression to express the role of Mary: Mother of God. This other expression is no longer concerned with God in the act of being born but expresses his personal relationship as God to the mother who gave form to his humanity.

The relation of the mother

I said 'gave form to his *humanity*', not merely his body, for a mother is not just a machine to fabricate a body, as an assembly line fabricates automobiles. She enveloped the body with all her human warmth and tenderness. After the birth, she introduced the little human animal to humanity. Without this, he would only be a wolf-child, as happens to children who have been abandoned.

The mother then watched over the psychological development of the little person, and thus he humanised himself. He learned to see in her his first human contact: she who had formed him and loved him. She taught him to love completely, with the demands, the momentary frustrations, the bursts of enthusiasm, the exchanges and choices of love. All that is realised through physical contacts beginning with nourishment: feeding at the breast, a profound experience of bonding for both mother and child.

In all of this, the Son of God learned humanity: a new

experience for God. Man is a being who only lives by eating and dies if he is not nourished. It is truly a matter of life or death and the Lord was mindful of this in instituting the Eucharist. All of this is much more important than it appears to be. In certain American clinics during the thirties when the cult of cleanliness resulted in babies being reared in incubators and attended to by gowned and masked nurses these children died off like flies or remained idiots. It is important to be stimulated by human affectivity through human encounters in order to become a man. Each child owes that to his mother. The Word of God learned it from his mother. He learned everything having to do with humanity from her.

Some serious objections

But, some object, why say 'Mother of God'? This is a mistake, and even a blasphemy:

— A mistake, since Mary, a creature of God, did not beget God. He pre-existed her.
— A blasphemy, since you make Mary into a goddess. Some historians of religion say that the Church has actually made her a goddess. It becomes clear that the contrary is the case when we see how the early Christians' disdain of cosmic divinities explains their extreme discretion regarding the Virgin Mary. They emphasised admirably the difference between these cosmic divinities, a fertile incarnation of the powers of nature, and this woman, servant and poor, who became the human mother of the incarnate Word. The clever concern by which they envisaged every type of confusion in this particular regard is quite commendable.

The defence of the title of *theotokos* was not aimed at promoting Mary but at maintaining the personal *unity* of Christ.

What the Council of Ephesus condemned is the dissociation of Christ: if it is not God who is born and who died for us, God and man are separated, juxtaposed but not one in Jesus Christ. Salvific love is emptied of meaning. Jesus becomes a mere puppet with God pulling the strings. He is not God made man. The fact that God assumed this human nature, this human existence in which he suffered and died, shows the folly of God's love for man. If this is not recognised, faith and salvation are on the rocks.

But weren't the Greeks right in defending the transcendence

of God? Is 'Mother of God' not perhaps a scandalous abuse of language?

Motherhood in reference to the person of the child

No, we are dealing with a human, anthropological and fundamental truth. A theologian who falsifies humanity falsifies God who made us in his image.

Let us understand this properly. A father and a mother are not father and mother only of the physical elements with which they endow their child. The father is the father of the spermatozoa and the mother is the mother of the ovum. This apparent logic would be inhuman and at the same time stupid, for maternity, like paternity, refers to the person of the child. The father and the mother are (together and correlatively) the father and the mother of Dominic, or of James, in person, and not of the body of James or Dominic.

The son of Mary is a divine person

Mary, like any other mother, is the mother of the person of her son, and her son is the Son of God in person. He is a pre-existing person, a divine person. Mary is indeed Mother of God in person.

It is essential to understand the first personal relationship of the Son of God with humanity, the first relationship with concrete and personalised love which he entered into by becoming man.

In the case of every infant, the mother is the first human relationship from whom he discovers all of the others, everybody else. For God, also, the first interior relationship to humanity was maternal. From the human point of view, a gift of God is necessary so that a woman can worthily and adequately establish this first relationship.

Mother of God in his humanity

But it is important to add: Mary is Mother of God in his humanity. She did not give birth to a divinity, but she had been chosen to give God the corporeal existence that he wished to assume in order to become one of us: 'For us men and our salvation', as the Credo states. It is by means of this adventure of God that we can understand his love for us and his plan of salvation. He concretely takes on total human existence, but without diminishing or downgrading his transcendence, without altering his divine existence as such.

Let us be quite clear about the fact that in no way does this make Mary a goddess. In this 'admirable exchange' she specifically represents humanity. And it is by virtue of humanity that she gives to God what he does not have. Some will object that he had everything. But what was lacking for the work of salvation was littleness, the capacity to act, to suffer, to die as a man in solidarity with humankind for its salvation. This has been expressed wonderfully by Marie-Noël in a poem in which Mary says:

A mouth, O my God, You do not possess
To speak to the damned here below,
Your mouth filled with milk turned toward my breast,
O my Son, it is I who have given it to you.

A hand, O my God, You do not possess
To cure with the wave of a finger their poor bodies
Your hand, closed like a ball, and still rosy
O my Son, it is I who have given it to you.

Flesh, O my God, You do not possess
To break the bread of a meal with them
Your flesh fashioned in my Springtime
O my Son, it is I who have given it to you.

Death, O my God, You do not possess
To save the world... O sorrow, here below
Your death by men, one black forsaken evening,
My little one, it is I who have given it to you.

B. Virgin

We have begun to understand why Mary had to be a virgin. This is in keeping with the transcendence of the Son of God, with his eternal and primordial relationship to the Father and with his singular relationship to this mother.

Certainly, this birth was a real birth, by which God became truly man but without any alteration of his transcendence. It was important that this transcendence be manifested in the bodily and psychic immanence of God in humanity. A biological father would have obscured the revelation of Christ, eternal Son of one single Father in a single filiation. In his case, as Matthew 1 has shown, human paternity could only be adoptive.

A sign

A sign had to be given that this human generation of the Son of God was beyond nature, coming from a transcendent God, and at the same time in accordance with nature, by his authentic insertion into humanity, material and maternal.

Matthew 1-2 and Luke 1-2 placed the virgin birth at the centre of the infancy narratives (although in a very different way). They knew it as a *fact*, not as an idea or deduction (a *theologoumenon*, as is alleged). Xavier Leon-Durfour and G.M. Soures Prabhu have provided solid historio-critical arguments regarding this.

A fact

The evangelists were surprised by this fact which revealed itself in the course of their inquiry. It went totally against accepted notions and against their very plan of action. This plan was to prove that Jesus was entitled to the designation Messiah, 'son of David' according to the prophets, and that the crowds were correct in acclaiming him as 'son of David' (*Matthew 9:27; 15:22; 20:20-31; 21:9,15;* cf *Mark 10:47-48* and *11:10*), through Joseph, an obscure descendant of David. But the investigation into family sources (at Jerusalem for Luke and perhaps at Nazareth for Matthew) taught them that Joseph was not the biological father of Jesus. This short-circuited their plan and their attempt to prove their theory. To rediscover it, it was necessary for them to reflect at great length and discover that Jesus was Messiah, *less as son of David* (by adoption) *than as Son of God*.

The evangelists propounded this profound truth which was so contrary to Jewish and pagan opinion. The affirmation of a virginal conception was, no less than in our time, an object of derision. Jews and pagans (Celsus, in the second century) would speak of adultery.

Theologically, the evangelists understood this mysterious fact on the basis of the gift of God: Christ, Son of God, 'God with us', (*Matthew 1:23*) and of Mary, his mother, model of consecration by the Spirit (*Matthew 1:18-20* and above all *Luke 1:35*), willing virgin prepared by God for this consecration (*Luke 1:34*).

The evangelists knew how to speak of this new truth, outside of the fashionable models with which they have been unduly identified to the detriment of their intentions. They avoided anything which could have compared this mystery with theogamies (erotic marriages) of gods and of goddesses.

They did not make of Mary the spouse of God (they only speak of her as the virgin spouse of Joseph). In the account of the virgin birth, they avoid speaking of God as Father (even though they will do so throughout the rest of their gospel), for God is not the human father, the biological father, the fecundator, in terms of the model of cosmic religions, or of distorted psycho-analytical interpretations of our gospels. Mary is no longer called 'spouse of the Holy Spirit', according to a questionable medieval formula. If both gospels refer the virginal conception to the Holy Spirit, the choice of this name of God goes back in one sense to the fact that the *spirit* (ruah) is feminine in semitic languages. This radically does away with every trace of a theogamy. The Holy Spirit is presented not as fecundator (as is the case with the interpretations by Jones and other psychoanalysts) but as a witness to the transcendent, truly divine origin of the son of Mary.

In short, they have expressed a new truth in an original manner: the coming of the Son of God without a biological human father, based on the startling information which they had gathered together from family tradition and from Mary herself (*Luke 2:19* and *51*).

This affirmation of both infancy gospels is confirmed by the whole of the New Testament in which Jesus never referred to any father other than God. Mark and Paul, the only ones who do not mention the virginal conception, explicitly avoid naming Joseph. Paul speaks of Jesus 'born of a woman' (not of a man). As for John, he considers, from a single perspective, the progression of the eternal birth, always virginal, in time, through the incarnation of the Word made flesh and by the baptismal birth 'Neither of water, nor of the flesh, nor of the will of man, but of God' (*John 1:13*).

Critical tenacity

This evangelical dogma, this humanly disconcerting truth that Mary is virgin and mother, has been the object of relentless criticism for over two centuries. There is no other dogma against which so many methodical, systematic, constant and ingenious efforts have been made to undermine this precious truth which is obscured in the minds of Christians themselves.

This disintegration is based upon some very particular, systematic and impassioned cultural presuppositions: those of rationalism (which is today losing its vitality), those of idealism which devalues the order of concrete realities and, finally, the setting up of sexuality as a supreme value and fundamental human right, reduced to libido as our fundamental, psychological constituent element. I have written elsewhere about these constant manoeuvres against the virginity of Mary and their internal contradictions.

— So-called scientific exegesis, in the name of textual criticism, first of all attempted to deny the authenticity of the passages which affirm Mary's virginity. But this science has eliminated these hypotheses and maintained these passages.
— There has been an attempt to interpret and explain them differently in various subtle and contradictory ways. Some have attempted to turn them into the mythologies with which the prevailing atmosphere of the time was filled, even though it is evident that they are so totally different from the Apocrypha.

Now is not the place to turn once again to this complex history nor to the analysis which can be found in varying degrees in the infancy narratives. Much has been said in the name of sexist or feminist ideologies: the virginity of Mary is an insult to the creative plan of God, to sexuality and to family. For God not to be born in a normal manner, for him to be an infant without a father diminishes his authenticity and his very humanity. This dogma only expresses the 'repression of celibate clerics' and 'the despisal of the noble relation between man and woman'.

— The family is not devalued since the Son of God was raised in a human family in which Joseph played the role of an adoptive father and we will see that adoption is not a reduced maternity or paternity.
— There is no longer any devaluation of sexuality. It is one of the most precious values of creation, essential to human communion as well as to the survival of humanity. According to God's plan, love between two human beings is necessary: between one man and one woman in order to create a new human person. If there is a different morality for Christ, it is because the birth of the Son of God is something else. His parents did not have to give him personal existence because he pre-existed. He came as God among men and received humanity for that purpose. In order to accomplish

this, God chose parthenogenesis, as scandalous as it might be for the wise and the clever, and as shocking as it was, as we have seen, for both evangelists.

The fathers of the Church had a profound perception of why the incarnation of the Son of God demanded the virginity of Mary. Father Terrien SJ gathered together their texts at the beginning of this century and summarised them all in this famous maxim:

> If a God had to be born, he could only be born of a virgin and if a virgin had to give birth, she could only give birth to a God (St Augustine, *De Trinitate*, 13, 18-23).

Sign of the unique divine filiation
This is a paradoxical thesis, but the dogma which expresses the transcendence of God often has an air of folly and audacity about it (cf *theotokos*).

The Fathers express it under different forms, like myriad sparkles coming from the facets of a diamond. They repeat that the virginity of Mary shows that the person of the Son of God could only have one father.[14]

Tertullian (+ 220) declared:

> If Christ is born of man, it is clear that it is from a virgin, otherwise he would have two fathers: God and a man, in which case the mother would not be a virgin (Tertullian: *Ad Marionem* 4, 10, 7, c2, 563).

And Lactantius, who died after the year 307, wrote:

> In order that he might appear, even in his manhood, as the Christ come down from Heaven, he had been created without the work of a father, for he had God for a spiritual Father; and as his spiritual Father is God, without there being a mother, likewise his bodily mother is a virgin, without there being a father (Lactantius, *De Divinis Institutionibus* n, 27, PL 6, 524).

In the same fashion, Proclus, in the fifth century, wrote that one single son could not be born of two fathers (Sermon 1, *on the Nativity*, n 3, PG 65, 713) and he specifies:

> The One who is without mother in the heavens is without father on the earth (*ib* 716). One and the same (Son) is

> without mother as Creator, without Father as creature (*ib* 685).

These affirmations express the fundamental truth that Christ had only one father and one divine sonship, to which Mary is related by the Incarnation. And it is in this line that we grasp the entire depth of the title of Mother of God.

Sign of transcendence

For the Fathers it is also a sign of transcendence:

> The Creator Word takes bodily form from a virgin, in order to give to all of us a clear proof of his divinity; for the one who has done this (it is necessary that he) is also the Creator of all the others (St Athanasius, *Discourse on the Incarnation*, no 18, *PG* 25, 128).

Sign of pre-existence

According to Theodotus of Ancyra it is a sign of the pre-existence of Christ which explains how the two births do not split the unique Son of God:

> Since the unique Son of God is born of the Father, how can he be born anew of the Virgin? He is born of the Father by nature, he is born of the Virgin by economy: in the former case as God: in the latter case as man (*On the Nativity of the Lord*, 2, no 7-8; *PG* 77, 1377).

Theodotus develops, at great length, a comparison:

> My Word (my thought) stems from my intelligence. But if I wish to write upon the paper, it is no longer the origin, the birth of this word, but only its visible manifestation. Likewise when the Virgin gives birth to the Word through her body, she doesn't give a begining to divinity by her travail. Not at all! But she makes God made man appear to men (*ibid*).

This comparison once again expresses the understanding that we already spoke about on the level of love. If the coming together of human loves is necessary for the creation of a new human person, the same no longer applies to the manifestation of the Son of God.

G. Martelet attempts to analyse more precisely the necessary connection between the Incarnation and virginity by showing that ordinary generation would transform the Incarnation into an adoption:

> If Jesus were the result of the love of Joseph and Mary, as great and holy as this love would have been, the fruit would have also been uniquely human... Undoubtedly this human fruit would have immediately been able to be appropriated by God, by virtue of an astonishing act of adoption which would have been so to speak, instantaneous! We would have had nothing else than a little man, become Son of God, adopted as they say and therefore only adoptive. In no way would we be before the mystery which Scripture reveals and faith confesses: that of the only Son of the Father become Man by the Incarnation (G. Martelet, *L'au-delà retrouvé*, Paris, Desclée, 1975, p. 203, note 8).

Sign of the new creation

The virgin birth is the sign which begins the new creation, announced by the prophets: a new world, beyond sin, beyond the rules of this world. Like the first creation, the new creation could only begin with the intervention of God alone. The human and masculine initiative does not have its place in this out-of-sequence birth in which God is born in order to renew all things radically.

Sign of agape *which transcends* eros

In modern times, it is quite certainly the Protestant Karl Barth who restored, with great vigour, this obscured dogmatic evidence. This mystery expresses the gratuity of the primary and fundamental gift of the Incarnation — he explains:

> The man Jesus has no father. His conception does not come under common law. His existence begins with the free decision of God Himself. It proceeds from the freedom which characterises the unity of the Father and the Son, bound by love, that is to say, by the Holy Spirit. This is the domain of the freedom of God, and it is from this freedom of God that the existence of the Man Jesus Christ proceeds.

This theologian, who had difficulty in coming to terms with the flesh finds, in this, the triumph of agape over eros. He testifies to this in a striking way:

> In every natural generation, it is man, conscious of his power, strong in will, proud in his creative power, autonomous and sovereign man who is in the foreground. The natural generative process would not then be a sign adequate to the mystery that is here to be disclosed... sexual union... could never be considered a sign of the divine agape, which is completely disinterested love. The will to power and domination that is present in man and finds expression particularly in the sexual act suggests something radically different from the majesty of the divine mercy. This is why it is Mary's virginity and not the union of Joseph and Mary, that is the sign of Revelation and knowledge of the mystery of Christmas. The history of humanity ... is in fact a history of males, a history of masculine exploits and undertakings... in this perspective, one may better grasp the sign of the mystery of Christmas in all its significance. The fact that Jesus has no human father deserves attention. Man, conscious of his will, and his power — man creator and master — would be incapable of participating in the work of God... consequently, the male must be excluded when a sign becomes necessary to reveal the inner dynamic of the Incarnation.

Without doing insult to the sexuality created by God in accordance with the law of love, in order to become a supreme expression of human love according to the flesh, this incisive testimony needs to be given pride of place so that animal sexuality may be accepted, governed and transfigured by human love and can participate in the creative act of God.

Sign of gospel poverty

The virginal conception still manifests itself right at the beginning of salvation, an essential aspect of the gospel of Christ: the good news announced to the poor, with poor means, worthy of God alone. God deliberately renounced the things of this world (riches, royal power, etc) with a radicalness which the Church had great difficulty understanding and accepting over the centuries. Thus Christ renounced:

— *royalty*, on the political level, in spite of the pressure of the crowds (*John 6:15; 18:36* etc).

— *money*, which he excluded from the preaching of the gospel:

'No coppers in your purses' (*Mark 6:8-9; Luke 9:3* and *10:4*).
— the self-satisfying *knowledge* of the scribes and Pharisees, whose schools he did not frequent. He spoke 'with authority' (*Mark 1:22, 27; John 7:46*) but in a different extraordinarily popular tone, which assured the lasting success of the gospel. And we must not forget fasting, which he practised at the beginning of his ministry, and to which Christians are invited, when 'the bridegroom is taken from them' (*Matthew 9:15* and *Acts 13:2-3*).

All these abstinences are considered foolish from the point of view of the wisdom of this world.

The virginal conception, the point of departure of God's own existence, manifests the most paradoxical sign of evangelical poverty: the sacrifice of sexual love.

Christ formulated this choice somewhat bluntly: 'making oneself a eunuch for the sake of the kingdom', and he commented, in the most laconic manner, about this strange suggestion: 'Let anyone accept this who can' (*Matthew 19:12*). The choice of celibacy for God alone is likewise as inexplicable, irrational and gratuitous as the choice, of every man or woman who marries, of one person of the opposite sex to the exclusion of all others.

The virginal conception, more shocking in the time of Christ than in our own day, in which knowledge has progressed in the area of parthenogenesis, only has meaning on the basis of God and of Christ.

Meaning for Mary

It has also a meaning for one whom Christian tradition calls 'the Virgin' par excellence. Mary is a prototype, the inventor of voluntary virginity. Is this to say that no one could have preceded her? No, for Philo knew communities of aged virgins living with the Essenes, as we have seen (pp. 2-9), but there we are dealing with ritual purity. Mary rediscovers virginity in accordance with love, as an exclusive and total gift to God. In this she is the first. She makes this choice before the Annunciation, as has generally been understood, up until our century when some have attempted to discover subtle and contradictory meanings behind Mary's statement:

I have no knowledge of man (*Luke 1:34*).

This statement, made in the present, signifies a resolution not to know as is the case when we say: 'I do not drink, I do not smoke', etc.

Mary was a 'voluntary virgin', through the light of God, as the Fathers are fond of repeating.

The fathers of the Church referred quite early to the example of Mary who had made this choice out of a super-abundance of love and freedom. They did not see in this an activity which would distance her from the rest of humankind but a sublime choice, a model to inspire them.

> *She conceived Christ in her heart* (by faith), *before doing so in her body*, they stated in various ways (a doctrine taken over by the Second Vatican Council, *Lumen Gentium*, cf. 8, n. 53, with references to the fathers of the Church).

Her virginity is first of all her pure faith, which inspired a total giving of herself to God which would also include her body. This gift is not sterility, but the principle of a new fecundity, the hundredfold of the gospel. Virginity embraced in charity amplifies love for others. Mother Teresa is a modern illustration of this.

For Mary there was something more, something unique. This virgin was mother in the fullest sense of this word: Mother of God and mother of men, her brothers, according to Christ's words on Calvary: 'This is your mother' (*John 19:25-27*). In that regard Mary is an example. Her exclusive choice has made her a mother a hundred times over, and she teaches all Christians, whether married or single, whether they are single by choice or in spite of themselves. She teaches them the faith which inspires and makes all states of life capable of bearing fruit.

The fathers of the Church clearly identified her faith and her virginity: the virginity of her faith refers her to God, as much as the integrity of her bodily virginity, one being the sign of the other.

Integral virginity

The Church very soon became aware that Mary, virgin par excellence, was integrally and totally a virgin 'before, during and after giving birth', in other words 'ever Virgin' (*aeiparthenos*). The Church therefore affirms that Mary, virgin when she conceived, has remained so, perfect in every way, on both the bodily and spiritual level. The birth of Jesus has not diminished but consecrated her virginity, as an ancient liturgical antiphon cited by the Council so beautifully and so poetically puts it (*Lumen Gentium* 57).

Later Mariology frequently focused upon anatomical details and descriptions which proved to be embarrassing and debatable. These descriptive efforts have the double difficulty of forcing open the doors of a mystery about which revelation does not provide us with many specifics. Such efforts are frequently lacking in decency. It is even more important to avoid recent debates, overly concerned with precise details, which have actually damaged the essential by confusing it with the superfluous by once again considering the gruesome descriptions of Tertullian about the violent birth of Christ which are so totally contrary to the whole of Christian tradition. This is a paradoxical novelty at a time when obstetrics seeks to promote painless childbirth for all women.

Let us respect the mystery of the virginal integrity of Mary and let us understand this, as scripture and the Fathers do, with reference to her virginal faith. Mary is the prototype of virginity, the one who truly expresses it in its most perfect form, the deepest and the most fruitful that has ever seen the light of day.

Virgin and Mother of God

Mother of God and Virgin still holds. Those who wanted to eliminate the virginity of Mary have generally, at the same time, and to the same degree, lost sight of the divinity of Jesus.

It can seem strange to affirm such a correlation for abstractly, theoretically and scholastically, it appears to be excluded. The Incarnation is defined by the sole fact that God assumes humanity. Whether he is born of a virgin or a couple does not change anything in the essence of the Incarnation. But a view which loses the virginal dimension of the Incarnation obscures or empties this mystery, in accordance with a deeper logic than that of abstractions. When I made this point about a quarter of a century ago, some theologians, who were friends of mine, talked me out of it: it was illogical! But since then, new illustrations have only served to confirm this correlation which was analysed above by Father Martelet.

The fathers of the Church sometimes expressed this logic by saying: the Son of God became what he was not (man), without ceasing to be what he was (God), and Mary became what she was not (mother), without ceasing to be what she was (virgin).

The paradox of virginity is a paradox of the transcendence of God made man among men.

Scientific problems

But which aspect makes this dogma paradoxical in the light of science? Today's biology, which has realised parthenogenesis in ever more and more advanced states, even among mammals, gives this virginity of Mary a new probability which, for all of that, does not allow us to reconstitute the model of this unique and mysterious event. For science can only study experimental and repeatable phenomena and we have no means of responding to the special questions which this mystery raises.

Normally, the product of a parthenogenesis would have to be feminine. How is it that the Son of Mary is of masculine sex? Perhaps one day biology will find the meaning to respond to this question by finding the element which opens the door to parthenogenesis.

Professor Lejeune, of the Academy of Medicine, a biologist of the highest level, who was asked by a priest if the virginity of Mary was rejected by science, responded by the following invitation to greater respect for the Mystery and a better understanding of science.

> If life is indeed, as we are taught today, the outcome of a message contained in DNA (the chromosomes, etc), then the Incarnation is the outcome of a complete message of the entire Word in a certain place, in a certain time. When theologians discovered that this Incarnation of the Word required a first stage, that of a properly finished receptacle — whence the Immaculate Conception of Mary, they perhaps made the most important discovery in the history of knowledge, although we still do not understand it. As for the Incarnation of Jesus, it was the fruit of a new intervention of the Holy Spirit. Thus the message of life is found suddenly complete, the word of God becoming man while remaining God. To attempt to describe this operation of the Holy Spirit in terms of the structure of chromosomes, and the formula of nucleo-proteins and the splitting of cells, would in no way appear irreverent, but perfectly futile. At the level in which we find ourselves I mean: in the current state of ignorance,

this would not be like leaving no stone unturned in order to scale Olympus, but it would be like pretending to describe the functioning of a computer when one hardly knows how to count on one's fingers (letter of 17 February 1976).

Holy

The holiness of the Virgin, mentioned by the gospels of John and Matthew, is expressed in depth by Luke's gospel: Mary is 'the object, par excellence, of the favour of God, (*kecharitomene*, 1:28), consecrated by the Holy Spirit who came upon her (Luke 1:35), blessed among women (1:41), happy for having believed and, because of this, the place, par excellence of the fulfilment of the promises (1:45). Mary herself gives thanks to God alone for having done 'such great things' through her.

Doubts and suitabilities

Theologians who like to multiply ridiculous hypotheses sometimes posit a sinful Mother of God, namely an adulteress (*Pikaza*), like Mary Magdalene. These hypotheses are even more foolish than they are blasphemous! Theology must interpret the real events of salvation and not make a travesty of them. Mary Magdalene illustrates the holiness of repentant sinners. Mary, Mother of God, illustrates the original and complete holiness which is the basis of the new creation. Let us respect the facts of the history of salvation and the data of revelation.

If we examine them, in accordance with their own logic, we understand much better why this holiness of the Mother of God is appropriate and, undoubtedly, necessary. Of course the fall of the most marvellous of creatures, Lucifer, prince of this world, as he is called in scripture, manifests the possibility of sin in creatures who have been most highly endowed by God: *corruptio optimi pessima* (the corruption of the best is the worst). And the holiness of Mary is not prefabricated, but free. Mary had to be a worthy Mother of God. If the holiness of Mary was, in a sense, necessary, it was not a mechanical necessity, but an interior necessity. First of all, from God's point of view, he was concerned with choosing and endowing his mother fully with every gift since she was to be a necessary collaborator in his work of mercy. For this purpose God chose, not a creature of a higher state, a princess, an eminent person, but a humble woman who described herself as 'servant' (*Luke 1:38* and *48*). If God, who gave angels and men the gift of freedom, had been deceived by Lucifer, he was not deceived by the poor, he had not been deceived by Mary. No creature had ever responded so well to the love of God.

Becoming aware

Curiously, the Church was slower in becoming aware of the holiness of Mary than of her divine maternity or her virginity. In the east, the misogyny of a number of the Fathers, who saw in femininity the epitome of weakness and of the defects of humanity, could only with difficulty imagine that Mary did not have weaknesses as did the apostles. From Origen to Cyril of Alexandria (the great doctor of the divine maternity who seems, however, to have corrected this opinion), they included Mary in their generalisations about sin. Moreover, it is important to maintain that Christ alone is holy by himself, and that he is the redeemer of all: all others were sinners; for if they were not, they would have been beyond the pale of universal redemption by Christ.

In the west, the awareness was a little more rapid. Because of Pelagius, St Augustine addressed the question. The Bishop of Hippo, formed in the school of the Manicheans, was inclined, as were many of his Jansenist or Protestant heirs, to emphasise the hold of sin over humanity.

Pelagius, therefore, attacked Augustine on his weak point, by reproaching him for soiling with sin, not only the saints, but the Virgin Mary. But Augustine, imbued with a sense of Christian tradition, responded, without hesitation, by making an exception for Mary 'whom it is necessary to recognise as being without sin' (*De Natura et Gratia* 42 CSEL 60, pp. 263-264).

In a second stage, Julian of Eclana engaged in the same conflict on a more delicate point: not actual sin, but original sin in Mary. This Pelagian was the first to deny explicitly that Mary had experienced the hold of original sin: 'By the original condition that you attribute to her, you deliver Mary in person to the devil', he objected.

Certainly Augustine did not wish to hand Mary over to the devil, but he reacted, this time, without sufficiently mastering the depth of the question. He attempted to extricate himself by making use of an ambiguous formula which removes Mary from the devil, while maintaining (correctly) her redemption by Christ but without succeeding in explaining how she escaped sin. We do not hand Mary over to the devil through the condition of her birth because this condition itself is annulled by the grace of rebirth (*Opus Imperfectum Adversus Julianum* 4, 122; PL 45, 1417-1419).

This is the beginning of a long history, in which the doctrine of Augustine on original sin will yield more or less negative conclusions whenever the problem of the conception of Mary is raised. This problem will only be resolved in the nineteenth century, with Pope Pius IX's definition, 8 December 1854.

2. TWO RECENT DOGMAS
The Immaculate Conception (1854) and The Assumption of Mary (1950)

Having examined the triple biblical truth, Mary, Mother of God, virgin and holy, dogmatically proclaimed, in a formal (or equivalent) way by the Church before the middle of the fifth century, let us pass to another stage: the two dogmas defined in modern times by Pius IX (1854) and Pius XII (1950): the immaculate origin of Mary and her Assumption.

Both of these dogmas have this point in common: that a formal biblical basis has not been found for them and that they cause ecumenical difficulties for our separated brethren. They have a less evidently christological, less central and more peripheral character and they have been defined during a pre-ecumenical period distinguished by the Counter-Reformation and the marian movement. This is dogmatic boldness, an extreme expression of Latin fervour during a period, deliberately closed, generous and concentrated around Mary.

These, however, are dogmas. If it has not been easy to establish properly their foundation, meaning and limits, they nevertheless shed light not only upon the beginning and the end of the Mother of the Lord but also upon the understanding of God's plans as they are manifested in the Bible. It is in this spirit that we must study them.

Let us once again take up the thread of the debate regarding the original holiness of Mary which was raised, for the first time, by the Pelagians against St Augustine, and which will arise again with the feast of the Immaculate Conception, in the Middle Ages.

The immaculate origin of Mary

History

The feast of the Immaculate Conception arose in the seventh and the eighth centuries, in the east, and homilists speak of the 'holy' and 'immaculate' 'conception' without raising those problems which were raised by the Latins.

The eastern feast passed into the west during the Middle Ages. From the ninth century, some monasteries in Germany and even at Rome adopted it out of a sense of piety and without reflection or discussion.

This feast was carried into England by monks around the year 1060, but disappeared at the time of the Norman Conquest in 1066. It was re-established on more reflective foundations in 1127 and 1128, and, from there, passed very quickly into Normandy and throughout Europe, in spite of St Bernard's opposition to this 'novelty'.

This fervent movement was not enlightened, and was shot-through with the confused ideas of the period. It was thought at that time, following St Augustine, that the sexual act (even in Christian marriage) was a disorder which transmitted original sin. One did not see how Mary, born of a father and of a mother, could escape it. Likewise, the very notion of conception was mixed up with pre-scientific notions at work at that time: a distinction was made between the conception of the body and the conception of the soul, so that it was believed that the soul was infused in male children before the fortieth day but, given the imperfection of their nature, this took place a little later for females.

To this was added an even more serious difficulty which theologians debated for a long time: Christ is Redeemer of all humankind. If Mary were exempt from all sin including original sin, Christ would no longer be the perfect Redeemer: the universal Redeemer of humankind. The nature of the Redemption would truly be changed. All the great scholars of the thirteenth century posited some stain of sin, at least in Mary's flesh, on the occasion of her conception.

It was to the credit of Duns Scotus at the end of the thirteenth century that he overturned the decisive argument according to which the immaculate origin of Mary did damage to the perfection of the Redeemer and the Redemption.

No, quite the opposite, Scotus responded. This manifested

the perfection of the Redeemer since the very perfection of the perfect Redeemer demands that he be able not only to cure sin but to prevent it. In fact, a mother who cleans off her infant who has fallen into mud demonstrates her efficacious love but if she prevents his falling into the mud she demonstrates an even more efficacious love. This profound intuition unblocked the insurmountable opposition to the original holiness of Mary which no one would have been capable of affirming up until that time. Scotus was content to show the *possibility* and appropriateness of the immaculate origin of Mary. If he had formally affirmed it, he would not have escaped condemnation.

After Scotus, the doctrine 'of original preservation' spread like wildfire so that by 1439, the Council of Basel defined it as an article of faith, but at a time when Rome considered this council schismatic.

The definition of Pius IX

It was after long centuries of controversy during which the Holy See, above all, sought to moderate violent differences, that Pius IX defined the immaculate origin of Mary. He did so in terms taken from his predecessor Alexander VII (1661), who very carefully explained the connection between the new dogma and that of *universal redemption*. He does not contradict this dogma but presents the immaculate origin of Mary as the explanation and special illustration of this fundamental dogma: Mary is indeed redeemed by Christ in the expectation and retroactive application of his merits.

> From the first instant of her conception, by a singular and privileged grace of Almighty God and in consideration of the merits of Jesus Christ, the Saviour of the human race, the Virgin Mary was preserved intact from every stain of original sin (Pius IX, Bull *Ineffabilis Deus*, 8 December 1854).

The ecumenical problem

This dogma, defined at a moment in which the Latin Church was culturally very isolated and had no other ecumenical preoccupation than the condemnation of heretics, has remained a difficulty for non-Catholic Christians: not only Protestants, but Orthodox and this for a number of different reasons:

— The Protestants (who follow the lead of St Augustine) stress the importance of original sin in humanity. That the Virgin would have escaped this seems to do violence to the transcendence of Christ the Saviour.

— The Orthodox, on the contrary, have a tendency to minimise original sin: St Irenaeus thought it was the error of youth. They feared that the dogma diminished the freedom, the 'feat' and the merit of Mary, to use a formula of Dean A. Kniazeff: an argument which is at the opposite pole from the Protestant argument.

It is a curious thing that dialogue with the Orthodox on this point is often more fraught with difficulty than dialogue with Protestants. The cause of this is not only the cultural distancing and the hurts which have provoked objections against everything which comes from Rome, but the estrangement which results from it with respect to their own tradition, for the eastern tradition affirms the original holiness quite strikingly, under forms very different from those of the Latins. For the Orthodox, Mary is, quite simply, holy origin, point of departure of the new creation, and this is affirmed poetically without dispute or emotion. For the Latins, on the contrary, the analysis on the confused cultural level results in the dominance of the negative opinion until the middle of the seventeenth century when the Holy Office was still applying sanctions against the Immaculists with the famous decree of 1627-1644. To the extent that Rome inclined in favour of the immaculate origin of Mary and then defined it, the Orientals stressed the negative sources of their tradition.

The feast of the Immaculate Conception, however, came to us from the Orientals and it was celebrated by them as the Holy Conception (unsullied). This is one of the numerous misunderstandings between our two traditions which differ as much as the right hand differs from the left — they are not interchangeable in spite of their identity of form and the manner in which they complement each other.

— In our dialogue with Protestants, let us be very precise about the fact that Mary is redeemed, that this truth is an integral part of the dogma and that it illustrates in a very striking and radical fashion the Protestant adage: *gratia sola*. This dogma attests that in Mary all is grace, all is the work of grace alone, regardless of any merit on her part.

— In addition to demonstrating the misunderstandings and the proper thread of their own tradition, it is important to show the Orthodox that sin is not a factor in liberty and that preservation from sin does not in any way diminish Mary's freedom. If Christ did not escape temptation, Mary must have known it in the trials of Christ's birth and above all at the time of his death, on Calvary where certain Greek fathers made the disastrous judgement that she had, in some way, succumbed to it.

Do we need to reformulate the dogma?

On the day when an end is made to the misunderstandings which have hardened, in large segments of the Greek world, the integrity of the monasteries which supply the bishops, and the lay theologians who inherit this same orientation, it will be most important to think about redefining together our common tradition. To do this it will be necessary to step back from this ambiguous and confused notion of *conception* in which the Latins have become entangled over the centuries. It would be important to speak of the holy and immaculate origin of Mary, to consider her, according to the eastern tradition, in a less analytical, less pointed manner than the Latins: as the first seed of the new creation, foretold by the prophets and fulfilled at the dawn of the New Testament, in accordance with Matthew 1-2 and Luke 1-2. At the Council, Bishop Butler attempted such a reformulation of the dogmas.

In this way, he was accepting the eastern theme of the 'purification of Mary' on the occasion of the Annunciation, by specifying, with Greek tradition (the first representative of which is Gregory of Nazianzen: *Oratio* 38, 13 PG 36, 325B = Oratio 45, 9, *ib* 633C), that this catharsis neither indicates nor implies any sin or moral stain but signifies an increase of grace and the radical confirmation of Mary by virtue of the relationship as mother which she contracted with God. Thus, Gregory of Nazianzen spoke of Mary as '*pre*-purified' (*prokathar-theises*) by the Holy Spirit, body and soul (R. Laurentin, *Court Traité sur la Vierge Marie*, Post-Conciliar Edition, 1967, p. 129).

Biblical foundations

This dogma, it has been said, is not biblical. Some have attempted to make up for this by starting with the title given to Mary at the beginning of the Annunciation: *kecharitomene*, 'the object, par excellence, of God's favour'. This title, and its context, which makes of Mary the eschatological daughter of Zion, the new Ark of the Covenant, constructed by God himself, goes along with the meaning of the dogmas, without, in any way, entering into its formal explanation.

But the dogma appears to be much more formally involved in the major current of biblical revelation: from *Hosea 2* to the Song of Songs, the people of God is presented as his spouse. According to the first text of this series, *Hosea 2*, Yahweh stigmatises his people as an adulterous spouse (*2:4-7*). But later he takes her back again as a fiancée:

> I shall betroth you to myself for ever.
> I shall betroth you in uprightness and justice
> and faithful love and tenderness.
> Yes, I shall betroth you to myself in loyalty
> and in the knowledge of Yahweh (*2:21-22*).

As the story unfolds, the initial mention of adultery disappears progressively and only the espousals remain. In the Song of Songs God goes as far as to say:

> You are wholly beautiful, my beloved, and without a blemish (*4:7-8*).

This promise of God is not empty. Where could it be realised, if not in the one who had been chosen as the point of departure for Christ, the Church and the new creation? The Church itself is made up of sinners. It is in Mary alone that she is holy and without stain. The original holiness of Mary is therefore strongly and ineluctably postulated by sacred scripture.

This dogma also manifests how the 'new creation' announced by the prophets begins with Mary. She is the new Eve in this new creation: 'younger than sin, younger than the race from which she sprang' (Bernanos, *The Diary of a Country Priest*, 1936, pp. 256-265).

The Assumption

The feast

Like the dogma of the Immaculate Conception, that of the Assumption is explained in the prayer celebrating the feast devoted to this mystery. This feast of Mary's birthday (the day of her birth in heaven) began at the start of the fifth century in the east, and spread under various names: Ascension (or Assumption), Dormition, Passage to Heaven (*transitus*).

It only passed over into the west in the middle of the seventh century; and, as is always the case among the Latins, met with more discussions and uncertainties than among the Orientals. The opposition to the apocryphal accounts of the death of Mary, which had inspired this feast, gave rise to a number of misrepresentations. In the ninth century, Radbertus published, under the name of St Jerome, a writing which contested the bodily Assumptionof Mary: her soul had assuredly joined Christ at the end of her earthly sojourn but had the body followed? The Apocrypha were not a solid basis for affirming this. It was therefore important to be on one's guard. This objection, which dominated the Middle Ages, was admirably refuted around the turn of the eleventh to the twelfth century by an English monk in the tradition of St Anselm. This anonymous monk published under the name of *St Augustine*, who neutralised the authority of Pseudo-Jerome. Nevertheless his enlightened reasons concerning the development of the dogma carried weight. The controversy arose again, however, among the clergy in the seventeenth century. But there was no doubt at all regarding this among the Christian people at large.

The definition of Pius XII

Pius XII defined the Assumption on 30 November 1950. He had inherited a plan for the definition of the mediation of Mary, which had been inaugurated under Pius XI. But he was conscious both of the ambiguity of this notion, and of its standing in opposition to the formula of the apostle — *one mediator alone* (*1 Timothy 2:5*) — and the ecumenical scandal which would result from it. He was impressed by the objections brought to bear by the Holy Office: how can we speak of Mary as mediatrix of all graces? She could not be mediatrix of graces in the Old Testament, or of sanctifying grace, which is the **immediate** communication of the divine life and actuation of the soul by God himself. Under these conditions, how can one speak of 'universal' mediation?

Pius XII transferred the plan for the marian definition of mediation to the Assumption, which posed fewer problems. He defined it in extremely stark terms to which translations frequently fail to do justice. Even in the liturgy, *assumpta* is translated as being lifted up, when it would be better to say 'taken up by God at the end of her earthly sojourn'.

Pius XII chose to make his definition, not on 15 August, which was the day of her feast, but on 1 November, the feast of All Saints, in order not to separate Mary, the eschatological icon, from all the saints called to join her in her glorification in body and soul with the risen Christ. The brief definition is only two lines long:

> At the end of her earthly life, the Immaculate Mother of God, ever Virgin, was *taken* (*assumpta*) to Heaven body and soul in heavenly glory.

What Pius XII formally defined is the actual presence of Mary in the glory of the risen Christ. Nothing more.

Where, when, how? Intentionally, the Pope does not respond to any of these questions. He does not even specify if Mary died, as is customarily said, or if she did not die according to the hypothesis of Epiphanus, adopted by Pseudo-Timothy and some others.

Demythologisation

He had profoundly demythologised the dogma: he stripped it bare of the imagery taken from the Apocrypha and from paintings: vertical ascension, amid a cortège of angels. He prescinded from every image of transfer: he spoke neither of 'going up' nor 'high' nor 'low'.

The word *assumpta*, taken, is the very one by which the Old Testament becomes aware of survival in God after death. This revelation is late. The first witness seems to be *Psalm 73:24*. The poor psalmist, crushed by the enemies of God, who are powerful, rich and triumphant, ends up realising what lot awaits him after his sufferings:

> You will *take me* into Glory, he says to God.

This evidence is constant throughout the Bible: Henoch (*Genesis 5:24; Ecclesiasticus 44:16* and *49:15*) and Elijah (*2 Kings 2:3-10; Ecclesiasticus 48:9*) have been *taken* by God, at the end of their earthly sojourn. This grace is the destiny of all the righteous. This dogma is therefore expressed in the best possible language: biblical language.

The sole exception to the relative silence in this definition, is the accumulation of Mary's titles: Immaculate-Mother-of-God-ever-Virgin. These titles show the convergent reasons for the Assumption. She who had been preserved from all sin, the one whose body had formed the body of Christ, through her incorruptible virginity could not be abandoned to death and to the corruption of the tomb. She could not suffer its influence but she could only be taken up by the Son. After having shared his death by compassion, she had to share in his Resurrection.

Do we need to reformulate this dogma?

This 'privilege' had been questioned by the theological hypothesis of Rahner according to which all the dead rise at the end of their earthly destiny; for death makes them pass beyond time into the eternity of God which is simultaneous. Thus they escape that amputated state of 'separated souls'. This abstract deduction does not respond to Christian tradition. Schillebeeckx, another innovative theologian, considers it a 'crypto-heresy'.

Rahner's hypothesis is contained in a series of reactions against the excesses of the theology of privileges. An attempt has been made to reduce Mary's privileges to the common lot of all men. Every infant is conceived without sin, since he is not capable of committing a responsible act and therefore cannot sin, and all men experience the Resurrection at the moment of their death. These clever but one-sided and paradoxical hypotheses obscure some important aspects of tradition.

Among the Orthodox Pius XII's definition stimulated some unprecedented reservations: not a denial of the Assumption, a feast which we owe to them, but a reaction against Roman infallibility. They claim that the Assumption is the object of liturgical contemplation and is not a dogma necessary to salvation: a nuance which is theirs together with many Anglicans.

Conclusion

The unity of the beginning and the end in God's plan

Whatever the ecumenical difficulties, both dogmas, defined a century apart during this modern era, are complementary and coherent. If they are more peripheral and less essential than preceding dogmas, they are not without light. They show how the fullness of God's love for Mary, the fullness of grace which is appropriated to the prototype of Holy Church and of every

Christian soul, encompasses both its beginning and its end. Her destiny is thereby better understood: Mary precedes and inaugurates the Church, in all the stages of her life.

She precedes the Holy Church by her original holiness, without which the Church would not have been originally and integrally the Holy Church, for she is made up of sinners. Mary precedes the Church, and is on the scene at the birth of Christ and during his growth and development, and she is present right up until the moment of his death. She is present at the very moment at which Christ sends the Holy Spirit upon the primitive community (*Acts 1:14 2:1-12*) in order to establish the Church. She precedes the Church at the very moment of the glorification of Christ.

Thus Mary appears as the prototype of the Church. In her are made manifest:

— the marvellous kindness of God's gift at her conception
— and the fullness of anticipated glory which her perfect union with her Son required.

Thus the profound dialectic of the joyful, sorrowful and glorious mysteries, which define so well the destiny of Mary and the Church, is quite apparent.

And so, God's way of acting is evident so much more deeply. At the beginning of his major undertakings, he places an initial intensive perfection which announces the final perfection, beyond the vicissitudes of this world. It is beautiful and it is important to recognise with certitude, in Mary our model and mother, this initial and final perfection, mirroring that of Christ, and following the admirable design of God in which all of us share.

3. TWO NON-DEFINED DOGMAS

These defined and extremely succinct dogmas, as the starkness and brevity of both definitions show, do not exhaust our knowledge of Mary as found in revelation, as is made clear not only in scripture, but in the practice of the Church, both in the liturgy and in the attitude which underlies that practice.

In both these areas, Mary forms an integral part of Christian dogma without the Church having made any decision or dogmatic definition on this subject.

1. Mary's role in salvation

The foundation

To be Mother of Christ was, for Mary, less a privilege than a function at the service of salvation and it is undoubtedly because of this that she qualifies as a servant of the Lord. By becoming human through her, Jesus Christ became priest and victim. For God, as such, would not be able to be victim and to be priest, he needed to be human (*Hebrews 5:1*). Mary therefore had been called to cooperate in the work of Christ beginning with the human existence she gave him.

The meaning

Redemption is not a gift of God which falls from heaven, a paternalistic work in which God is the giver and we are merely receivers. God realised salvation, not from on high, but from within humanity, through a man, Jesus Christ, and he enlisted our cooperation at all its stages. Mary is to the forefront of this cooperation. In this she is still the prototype of the Church: redeemed in order to cooperate in the Redemption, step by step.

The steps

1 Mary cooperated in the very formation of Christ the Redeemer. She not only formed his body, she consented to this plan of God by an unconditional commitment of faith, hope and charity. She did not agree merely to conceive and bring forth a son (*Luke 1:3*), but to give birth to the Saviour, and to have common cause with him. Such is the meaning of her unconditional and irreversible *fiat*. She shared the entire hidden life of Christ, thirty out of thirty-three years.

2 Mary shared in the decisive hour of Christ's death. She represents there, in intimate and perfect union with him, the communion of a simple creature, a human person, one redeemed, a woman: playing the part of the new Eve in relationship to the new Adam. She is not another Saviour but represents communion and perfect cooperation with the Saviour. This corresponds well with the structure for communicating salvation as established by God: in the Mass, the priest alone receives the power to actualise the sacrifice of Christ, yet all communicate. Mary, prototype of communion in Christ, is also a prototype of the faithful at the redemptive sacrifice of Christ.

Mary participated sorrowfully in the Passion by her compassion as a mother and by being pierced (*John 19:34*), as predicted by Simeon (*Luke 2:35*). As she stood before the atrocious sufferings of her son, the cruellest torture of all for a mother, watching his unthinkable defeat and the apparent victory of Satan, at a time when these events could spark many a temptation — her irreversible *fiat*, which was so sorely tested, attained its supreme confirmation! Like the offering of the faithful at the sacrifice of the Mass, Mary's communion with Christ was integrated with the sacrifice which wrought our Redemption. It is in this way that she cooperates, through faith and prayer, in the pentecostal birth of the Church.

3 Mary today continues to cooperate with Christ in a perfect and glorified communion of thought and action. The Lord had inspired Thérèse of Lisieux to spend her heaven doing good on earth. Since this inspiration was certainly not a delusion for Thérèse, would it not have been given in abundance to Mary? According to the Church's conviction and deepest experience, Mary our mother continues to concern herself with her children, whom she now knows through the knowledge and glory of God.

An abundant vocabulary

In order to express Mary's current role, the manner in which she shares the saving action of Christ today, all sorts of titles have been coined:

— *Queen*, for she reigns with Christ, she shares his glory and his very power, as she shared his passion and his death, in accordance with the profound law of perfect communion: 'Everything which belongs to me is yours, everything which is yours is mine'. In no way does this diminish the divinity of Christ and his exclusive power as Redeemer, but it shows his admirable plan to have all of the redeemed share in it, beginning with Mary, a model of the Church.

— *Coredemptrix* (a term which arose in the fifteenth century, and which spread widely only at the beginning of the seventeenth century), once seemed to mariologists to be the most fitting term to signify Mary's cooperation in the Redemption and they sought to make a new dogma of this. But many theologians criticised the prefix *co* because it seemed to place Mary on an equal footing with the Redeemer. It did not show Mary's dependence upon Christ, or even the fact that in this redemptive sacrifice Jesus, alone, is the priest and victim of the sacrifice, since he alone died and rose again; only he ascended to heaven at the end of the sacrifice; only he is the adequate cause of the Redemption in which Mary communicated so perfectly. At the time when the title, Coredemptrix, seemed to be so close to dogmatic definition Cardinal Journet, who sensed the ambiguities of the word, attempted to dispel them by making them quite commonplace. He extended it to all Christians: Mary is Coredemptrix, and we are all coredeemers.

Since the Council deliberately did away with this term, it would seem to be more fitting now to stop using it and to specify Mary's proper role in such a way that it is neither confused with that of Christ the Saviour, nor with our own role in the working out of the Redemption.

— *Mediatrix* was the subject of a mighty campaign for definition, inaugurated by Cardinal Mercier, but abandoned by Pius XII, as we have seen. The Council set about explaining that whenever the Church employs this title, she does not intend to obscure the position of the sole Mediator. What this title attempts to convey is that Mary, who cooperated with grace in the highest fashion possible at the coming of Christ, cooperates in the diffusion of the graces flowing from his Redemption. She is in some manner the means (medium). Her intercession enables us to receive these graces and she is associated with Christ for the purpose of giving them to us. Today this term is avoided not only because it disturbs Protestants but because there are more felicitous ways to say the same thing and these have a serious biblical basis.

To their objection, taken from St Paul, 'Christ is "sole mediator"' *(1 Timothy 2:5)*, we can reply: Yes, but the apostles also say that 'Christ alone is Lord'. However, in the words of the Credo, the Father is also Lord and the Holy Spirit is Lord. Certainly, but you would be in error if you said: There are three Lords. No, there is only one Lord in three persons: the father is Lord, the Son is Lord, and the Holy Spirit is Lord, but they are one and the same Lord. Likewise the Father is God, the Son is God, the Holy Spirit is God, but there are not three Gods, there is one God in three persons. Let it not be said, therefore, as we saw in the writings of a reputable theologian: 'These two great Mediators, Jesus and Mary'. The Council states that 'If Mary is Mediatrix, it is through Jesus without increasing or adding anything to the dignity and the effectiveness of Christ the sole Mediator' (*Lumen Gentium* n. 62).

Theologians of mediation have attempted to resolve the ambiguities of the vocabulary of marian mediation by stressing that 'Christ is sole Mediator of Redemption, but there are mediators of intercession'. But this distinction, proposed in the seventeenth century, was constantly being twisted. The Protestant pastor, Hans Asmussen, would have accepted the title of Mediatrix by specifying: 'Mediatrix in Christ', for we are mediators in Christ, the sole Mediator.

— *Auxiliatrix* is a title accorded to Mary by John Bosco, taking his lead from the fathers of the Church. Mary, who had assisted Christ in the initial conception and formation of his humanity, aids and assists her other children as we journey on the road to divinisation. This is a result of her role in 'the admirable exchange'.

Our mother

Mother of Christians, more broadly, *mother of men*, *our mother*, is the title the Council (*Lumen Gentium Ch* VIII) insists on, since on Calvary she accepted the vocation of mother, which Christ intended for her. He had entrusted his disciples, and then all Christians to her but she is the mother of all who are *called* to become disciples of Christ.

The notion of spiritual maternity is true and it is beautiful, but it has its ambiguities. It is most important to do away with these, for our love of Our Lady, like our love of God, only needs truth. Truth both liberates and stimulates.

Sometimes we say Mother of God, then mother of men (or, better, Mother of God made man, therefore mother of men, his brothers). The conciliar text summarised this at the outset in the formula 'Mother of God and of men'.

Mary is Mother of God because she gave birth to the Son of God according to his humanity and she formed his humanity as every mother forms her infant. This is not true for other Christians. Each of them, each of us has our own mother who brought us into the world. Mary's motherhood has, therefore, an adoptive character. She is our spiritual mother in Jesus Christ in order to kindle divine life in us and guide us to the divinisation to which God calls us.

Certain theologians find the word 'adoption' repugnant since it seems to signify a reduced motherhood. This would be to misunderstand adoption as experienced in depth by mothers who adopted children either because they had none of their own or because these children were abandoned and they took them in along with their own. These generous adoptions are a marvellous adventure. And mothers who have experienced this frequently become aware of an essential dimension of maternity which not all mothers are capable of realising. An adoptive mother is a real mother, with the same feelings as a mother who has given birth and, for Mary, this psychological feeling is accompanied by a spiritual and divine sensitivity in accordance with the gift of God.

For this universal task, God enlarged Mary's heart, not only to the human capacity of mothers of large families, who sometimes adopt other children, but to the immeasurable capacity of God. He had given her a super-abundant capacity for her task on behalf of all men. For Mary, each of her children, each one of us, is unique and we can give thanks to her and to God for this.

This introduces us to the next and final point of the dogma.

2. Mary in worship

The final fact about Mary which comes from revelation is her place in Christian worship, in Christian prayer, in the daily life of the Church; this is a vast subject.

Origins

From the second century Mary had a place in Christian worship immediately after that of the martyrs, whom the earliest Christian generations celebrated as an integral part and prolongation of Christ in his Passion. Mary found her place in worship a little later but in a necessary and integral fashion.

We know very little about the earliest liturgy of the Church which was essentially oral worship, without missal, without paper, but solidly etched upon the memories of the people of that time.

The Magnificat undoubtedly formed part of the worship of the early Church at Jerusalem and Luke culled it from here. It attests to the fact that the primitive prayer of the Church had taken over Mary's prayer, the most outstanding prayer in this community (see above pp. 39-40).

Mary had her place in the thanksgiving bequeathed to this community: 'All generations will call me Blessed' (*Luke 1:48*). In singing this verse, the primitive community also gave thanks to God for the great things that he had done for Mary before he extended them to the Church. In short, the earliest of the Christian communities, one of the best known, extended Mary's thanksgiving to God alone, for the incarnation of the Saviour in whom were fulfilled the promises made to the people: to Abraham and to his descendants forever (*Luke 1:55*).

Prayer with Mary

This is only one example (but undoubtedly the earliest) of Mary's place in the liturgy, not a prayer to Mary, but a prayer *with Mary*, which is more important still.

Mary's place in worship is not limited to prayer *to* her, which is only a particular, secondary and relatively late form of her place in worship. The ancient rule of liturgical prayer, formulated at Rome during the fourth and fifth centuries, is to be addressed to the Father through Christ and this rule has been preserved, not only in prayers, but in the central part of the Mass: the *anaphora*, also called the Canon, in which Mary, from the end of the fourth century, had her own place. She is mentioned in the Greek Canon, adopted in the fifth century by the Roman Church and still in use: the first canon (canon of St Pius V), which inspired the others in which Mary also has her place. This is the *Communicantes*, right before the Consecration. It shows the undeniable place of Mary in the Incarnation and in the very birth of Christ, including this sacramental birth:

> in union with the whole Church, venerating, in the first place, the memory of the Blessed Virgin Mary Mother of our God and Lord Jesus Christ ...

Mary heads the list of the communion of saints.

In accordance with this model, Mary also has her place in several prayers of the Mass which are similarly addressed to the Father through Christ: never to Mary, never to the Holy Spirit, and only by exception in the Mass of the Sacred Heart, in which a prayer is addressed to Christ himself. Mary intervenes as an incentive for petition, or for imitation, or for intercession.

The sanctoral cycle
Mary's personal feasts are also a secondary, relatively late source of her place in worship (see below pp. 139-140).

The temporal cycle
It is in the mystery of Christmas that Mary first finds her proper place. The gospels of this feast were an occasion for speaking of her and people were preoccupied with explaining her role through all sorts of celebrations which preceded or followed Christmas, for example Advent, in which the gospels of the Annunciation and the Visitation have pride of place. Certain liturgies celebrate Mary, eight days before Christmas (18 December) and eight days after (1 January). This octave of Christmas, devoted to the virginity of Mary, a specific sign of the Incarnation, was obscured by 'the feast of the Circumcision'. At the conclusion of the Council, this feast was restored to its primitive meaning. It is, today, the feast of Mary, Mother of God.

The Byzantine liturgy shows the marvellous place of Mary in the mystery of Easter. The Latin liturgy is certainly poor by comparison. After the suppression of the feast of the Compassion which, before the Council, was celebrated on the Friday of the Passion, she occupies a discreet place in the liturgy of Good Friday. We read of her in the Passion according to St John, where the dying Jesus makes us children of Mary: 'This is your mother'.

We can rediscover Mary, in an equally biblical and discreet fashion, in the liturgy of Pentecost in which the Acts of the Apostles call attention to her presence at the heart of this mystery.

Finally, Mary had her place in the biblical feasts of Christ: in the announcement of the birth of the Saviour (Annunciation); and in the Presentation (which for a long time was known as the Purification of Mary), an ambiguous and awkward term, since the gospel of Luke had specifically avoided attributing this purification to Mary, transferring it instead to Jerusalem (*their* purification: *Luke 2:2*)). It has been re-named the *Presentation of Christ*. This new designation does not diminish, but revitalises, in accordance with its full significance, the role of Mary who bore and presented Jesus in the temple and then received, from Simeon, the twofold prophecy about the glory of the Saviour and about her being pierced by compassion.

Genesis of the prayer to Mary

From when does prayer addressed to Mary date? In the west, it is relatively late. St Augustine is unaware of it, although he may be said to be at the threshold of this prayer as he addresses himself to Mary in his sermon (280) on the *Nativity*:

> Who are you therefore, you who must give birth? From whence did this honour come to you? How will there be formed in you the very one who made you? From whence do I say such great good comes to you?

But this is not a prayer, it is *prosopopeia* (analogous to that which Jean-Jacques Rousseau addressed to Fabricius):

> I seem to be interrogating the Virgin and striking her ears as I importune ... Let the angel respond (Sermon 280, 11,6 *On the nativity of John the Baptist* 5; PL 38, 119).

We are faced with a similar situation whenever Augustine addresses this injunction to Mary which will be used as prayer in a very short time:

> Give us our bread, come from Heaven, placed in a manger, such is the nourishment of animals (Sermon 369, PL 39, 1655).

But from the first half of the fifth century, beginning with Sedulius, prayer to Mary appeared in poetic form:

> *Salve Sancta Parens enixa puerpera regem coelum terramque regi.*
> Hail, Holy Mother, giving birth to the king who rules heaven and earth (CSEL 10, p. 48-49).

Among the Greeks, prayer to Mary was already present in the homilies of the fourth century in which the salutation of the angel '*Chaire Maria*', 'Rejoice Mary', became a prayer addressed to her. This is also the case with a piece of *graffiti* in Nazareth which archaeologists date from the third century.

The second phrase of our *Hail Mary*, the equally biblical apostrophe of Elizabeth, 'of all women you are the most blessed, and blessed is the fruit of your womb' (*Luke 1:42*), is also repeated, beginning with the fourth century, as a prayer in the homilies.

A papyrus discovered in the sands of Egypt contains a well-known text which some believe to be of Latin medieval origin.

Palaeographers date it from the third century. Theologians have argued for a later date because of the fact that it contains the title of *theotokos*. But the objection is without value for the title was current in Egypt from the third century before spreading throughout the entire Church by the fourth century. If we can rely on the testimony of Socrates, which goes back to the fourth century (R. Laurentin, *Court Traité*, p. 170), Origen would have employed it in his lost commentary on the Epistle to the Romans. Here is this early prayer to the Virgin:

> Under the mantle of your mercy, we flee to you, *theotokos* (Mother of God). Do not cast off our demands but save us from evil. (You) alone who are chaste and blessed (papyrus no. 470 of the John Rylands Library, Manchester, object of an extensive literature beginning with Dom Mercenier, in Museon 52, 1939, pp. 229-233).

Prayer to Mary is secondary and marginal in the liturgy but we are not forbidden to converse with our mother in the communion of saints.

CONCLUSION

Such are the Christian dogmas concerning Mary. They have been mentioned one by one for greater clarity but it is not a question of a particular truth or of isolated dogmas. It is necessary and important to place them in a unified whole.

Unity of the mystery of Mary

Mariologists seek, above all, to locate these dogmas in the unity of the mystery of Mary. This mystery certainly has its own twofold coherence.

— Mary is the masterpiece of God, who chose this woman in order to bring his Son into this world, in order to communicate and cooperate with him in the plan of salvation, as the new Eve, prototype of the Church and of every Christian soul through her union with Christ, her godly life, and her charisms.

— Mary is also the most perfect response which has been given to God, the freest and most complete adherent and cooperator with his will, even to the point of a mortal trial on the occasion of the death of her Son.

Treatises on mariology have attempted to show this unity by formulating a 'first principle' of mariology, a starting point by which we would be able to deduce or at least clarify the inner logic of all the rest. These discussions have shed some light. Some experts have centred everything upon the divine motherhood, which is indeed the centre of the plan of God; others upon the association of the new Eve with Christ, her motherhood being but one aspect. Others have centred on Mary, as a type of the Church. A Protestant, S. Benko,[15] has proposed another principle: *Mary is the principle of the kenosis (the self-emptying) of Christ.* This principle can appear humiliating and less glorious and protestant (in the aggressive sense of that word). But Benko has correctly drawn this concept from St Paul in *Galatians 4:4*. And it has its own merit and truth. The fundamental mariological principle (if one wishes to designate it as such) of Grignion de Montfort is present here. It is this which gives balance and coherence to all his fervent thought; it is the very same principle by which Mary gave to God her own self-emptying (R. Laurentin, *Le Secret de Marie,* 1985, pp. 152-153).

The meaning of Mary in the unity of the Christian mystery
But other theologians think that Mary cannot be reduced to a principle. This would result in a closed, narrow mariology, disconnected from the rest of theology. The proper way of inserting Mary into Christian theology, they say, is to find a place for her in the various treatises or chapters of theology: her function as Mother of God in the *Treatise on the Incarnation*, her cooperation in Salvation, in the *Treatise on the Redemption*, her Assumption in *Eschatology*; her exemption from sin in the *Treatise on original sin*, where she is too frequently forgotten, and so on. This would certainly be the best way to teach about Mary. But, alas, in those faculties of theology where there are no specialised courses on Mary, Our Lady is usually largely forgotten. In order to remedy this condition, it will certainly be necessary, for quite a long time, to be resigned to writing treatises on the Virgin Mary in order to prepare for her re-insertion into the whole of theology.

She has her place there, totally connected to Christ, as de Montfort said, in fact, totally referred to Christ, in accordance with a dynamic and clear reference in the gospel of Cana as well as in the *fiat* of the Annunciation. She has her place in the unity of the mystery of Christ, which begins with her maternal role and continues with her cooperation and her communion which prefigures that of the Church. She therefore lays a necessary, undeniable and irreplaceable role in the plan of God and in all of Christian theology which will forget her only at the price of grave damage to the Church.

A theology in which Mary no longer has her own place becomes terribly abstract, masculine, inhuman. If God chose to be born of a woman, it was perhaps partly in order to keep theologians from getting bogged down in abstractions and misogyny. They should recall that Mary was the first to know Christ, whom she had formed humanly. We find excellent testimony about this in *Luke 1-2*. The account of the Annunciation, superb feminine theology, misunderstood and unappreciated, is not inferior to the prologue of John which repeats the themes in an abstract and masculine manner. Jesus' first acquaintance, namely that with Mary, was intuitive, existential and a personal acquaintance, but it was also bodily. Mary knew better than anyone the body of Christ which she had formed, as well as his mystical body of which she was the first charter member, committing herself to Christ by her *fiat*. Abstract and systematic theology, the key role of which needs to be recognised, is only a derivation of the intuitive knowledge of Mary and it is, moreover, in this precise sense that Leo XIII, for the first time, gave her the title of Mother of the Church, mother because she had given the apostles initial knowledge of the Incarnation and the infancy about which they had been ignorant until then.

In a real fashion, she is Mother and mistress of the Church and Queen of the Apostles, with whom she shared the divine oracles which she preserved in her heart: *Luke 2:19* and 51 (Encyclical *Adjutricem populi*, in *Acta Leonis XIII*, 15, p. 302).

Fortunately, during this year with Mary, the Marian Year, we are no longer speaking of 'marian dogmas' but of the place of Mary in the body of Christ: a necessary place because it was willed and chosen by God, irreplaceable in revelation and in Christian dogma.

4

HOW TO LIVE THIS YEAR WITH MARY
HER PRESENCE AND OUR CONSECRATION

We understand who Mary is. In history she is a poor woman, in whom there were divinely fulfilled all the values of the poor, the first individuals for whom the good news was intended. God exalted her poverty to the point of making her Queen of the angels, the Queen of the world and all creatures. In this way he elevated her, without altering her humility or her poverty. He did not remove her from nature but fulfilled her. He did not disfigure her but transfigured her. She is not a goddess but the prototype of this divinisation, respectful of our humanity, by which we are all called to follow in her footsteps.

Where are we going?

So much is clear, even if this mystery goes beyond us. But Mary is not an object to be displayed in a glass case. It is not enough to know that she is the masterpiece of God nor even to admire her. We need to enter into a personal relationship with her, to establish bonds with our mother who is also our sister since, in fact, she is one of us.

It is not a matter of producing a marian object always more marian but of meeting Mary. It is not a question of heaping up devotions, practices and a multitude of words. Of course words have their place since every love normally flourishes by means of words which, however, remain light and flighty even when they are so numerous and naive. But the essentials are the words themselves. This is what inspires beauty and authenticity.

Certainly, 'if devotion to the Holy Virgin distances one from Jesus Christ, it is to be rejected as an illusion of the devil' (Grignion de Montfort, VD no. 62, cf no. 225). But it is clear that Mary plays a part in the mystery of Christ and helps us to understand and serve him better. Such is the programme of this year with Mary, decided upon by John Paul II.

Discovering a presence

What is this about? Not so much about giving more glory to Mary, who herself seeks only the glory of God as her Magnificat attests. It is good to give thanks with Mary and for Mary. But it is above all a matter of properly perceiving, identifying and living out the bond that God has established between her and us, by prolonging the bond established between her and him, and of living out this bond, this relation, in the communion of saints in Jesus Christ.

To do this, we must first of all become conscious of her presence in order truly to give form to that presence in our midst.

We will, later on, attempt to understand the place and role of Mary in our consecration to God. This second point needs to be considered for several reasons:

— This consecration is a project of John Paul II and his predecessors.
— Since the time of Pius XII this project has been a sign of contradiction, not only between Fatimists and anti-Fatimists, but between its most ardent promoters as well as traditional theologians. This consecration seems to them to be uncalled-for on the basis of questionable vocabulary. This may explain why the consecration which John Paul II asked the bishops to make in all the dioceses of the world, on 24 and 25 of March 1984 has been so little heeded. Such hesitation had its own reasons which it is important to overcome in order to reconcile the Christian intelligentsia, concerned about theological precision, with the ardent fervour attendant upon the private revelations of Our Lady. What better occasion than this year with Mary for such a reconciliation?

1. PRESENCE OF MARY

Can we speak of a **presence of Mary**? The expression is justified and unambiguous (unlike many others in this field) and the foundations for it are sound. Mary is present at every Christian mystery and at all the periods of salvation (see below p. 66).

She holds first place next 'to Christ, and is closest to us', the Second Vatican Council declared (*Lumen gentium* n. 54). Right from the start she is the first member of Christ, the founding member of the mystical body, the most important, the most universal in the communion of saints, during Pentecost, at which she was present. She remains the summit and the ardent heart of the Church in Jesus Christ.

How do we become conscious of this presence? How do we actualise her presence? Why do we remain such poor lovers, we who are not so poorly loved?

Foundations

In order to grasp once again, from within, our bond with Mary and the body of Christ, we need to understand it, to find a basis for it and to evaluate it.

What, then, is the bond? How do we become conscious of it?

1. The presence of Mary in scripture

We find the model for this in scripture: as we have seen, Mary is present throughout the life of Christ. She made ready for him at the very high-point of the Old Testament which she concludes. She introduced him into the human family, unfolded his humanity, accompanied him throughout his hidden life until he reached the age of thirty. She became involved in his ministry by suggesting to him the sign of Cana (*John 2:1-22*). During the three years of separation, her spiritual communion deepened further. She was one with him physically and morally during his suffering and death on Calvary, through compassion with his Passion. She prepared for and accompanied, through her prayer, the birth of the Church (*Acts 1:14*). Finally, she rejoined her son in the glory of the Assumption.

She was present physically throughout the life of Christ (labouring, sorrowful and glorious), both by her mother's love and by her commitment to him. It was a communion of faith, of hope and of charity. Mary's presence to her son is a model for us, since through this mother, God becomes our brother and has given her to us as mother in order to identify us with himself.

Certainly, our filial connection is different from that of Jesus since Jesus is God. If he owes his humanity to her, she owes everything to him as God. We are humble children of this mother who has so profoundly and spiritually adopted us in him.

In accordance with the logic of this wonderful exchange, Mary, who gave human humility to the Son of God, has the mission of aiding the work of our divinisation in Jesus Christ. She cooperates with him in this work of God.

2. The presence of Mary in the liturgy

The liturgy (the official and constant prayer of the Church, the *lex orandi*) reflects this universal and discreet presence.

Mary, as we have seen, has a twofold place in both liturgical cycles: the temporal and the sanctoral, and at each Mass, in the *anaphora* which is its centre. This has been the case since the fourth century (see above p. 105).

United to her son in one and the same prayer, she knows, with him and in him, the Church and each one of us. She is at the service of her children entrusted to her by Christ. With him she intercedes and assists them. It is important to be conscious of this in living out the faith.

3. The presence of Mary in the life of the Church

Mary's discreet and universal presence continues throughout the life of the Church: visible and invisible, in its history, its churches, its religious art. The call for her intercession appears throughout the dogmatic history of the councils and the various complex struggles within the Church which, during the Carolingian era, inspired the famous antiphon:

> *Cunctas haereses interemisti in universo mundo*
> You have conquered all heresies throughout the world.

She was also the inspiration for the initiatives and victories of the Church. Many feasts were instituted in order to commemorate her efficacious assistance. From the earliest centuries, the most ancient churches were dedicated to her since she was the first temple of God and remains the model of all others. Mary, model of the Church, is also the model of the churches where the eucharistic presence of the Lord is renewed and where prayer takes place continuously.

In these churches, as in our homes, her images have their place:

— depictions of her praying which remind us of her prayer,
— icons of tenderness (*eleousa*), which recall to us her affective and maternal relation with Christ, but also with us.

They have stimulated faith and Christian fervour. In short, she has her place in the daily living-out of the Christian life.

4. *The discovery of the saints*

The truth of this presence has been experienced for a long period of time by the saints, who were able to discover her through a very deep and fruitful experience.

The first explanation of this presence goes back to St Ambrose. He comments, in this fashion, on the visitation of Mary to Elizabeth (*Luke 1:39-56*).

> The superior comes to the inferior in order to assist the inferior: Mary to Elizabeth; Christ to John, as later on, in order to consecrate the baptism of John, the Lord came to this baptism. Consequently, the value of the presence of Mary and of the presence of the Lord is apparent (*Exposition on the Gospel of Luke* 2, 22, PL 15, 1560c).

And in another commentary regarding the Visitation where Jesus and Mary manifest their presence dynamically:

> The presence of the *verbum* exercises a power, and likewise the presence of Mary (*presentia Mariae*), who bore him in her womb, instructs John, in the womb (of Elizabeth), to the point that, in the womb, he dances and exults with joy (*De Isaac* 6, 52; PL 14, 521c).

This is still merely a biblical reference to Mary's presence but for St Ambrose it has a symbolic value. These two texts seem to reflect the experience of her presence in the communion of saints.

Likewise, in the second century, when the *Protoevangelium of James* speaks of the child Mary entering the temple: 'She danced and all the people loved her'. This mention, which is without historical basis, conveys the love that the unknown author and the readers of this popular book had already demonstrated toward Mary.

But it is only at the end of the patristic era that Mary's presence is described as an experience. *Germanus of Constantinople* (c. 634-733) expresses this in the following prayer addressed to Mary:

> You who have cohabited completely with God, you have left this world, without abandoning those who were in the world

> ... We are accustomed to venerating you with faith ... We call thrice happy those who are enjoying your visible presence (*paroikias,* from *oikia*: house, habitation), and those who know how to find you as Mother of Life. As you marched with us bodily, so the eyes of our spirits are awakened each day to see you. Likewise you have cohabited bodily with those of the past (*cf John 19:27* and *Acts 1:14*), and thus you dwell with us in spirit (*pneumati synoikeis*). The powerful protection with which you cover us is the sign of your presence (*synomilian*) among us. We all understand your voice, and our voices reach your ears. We are all known to you because of your concern, and we recognise your powerful and permanent assistance. In no way, I say, can the separation of soul and body alter the human relation between you and your servants. You have not abandoned those you have saved, you have not left to their own devices those whom you have gathered together, for your spirit always lives and your flesh has not known corruption in the womb.
> You visit all (mankind) and your glance (*episkope*: oversight, vigilance) is over all, O Mother of God, although our eyes are impeded from seeing you. All holy, you dwell in the midst of us, and manifest yourself to those who are worthy of you ... You approach those who invoke you (Homily *On the Dormition*, p. 98, 344d, 345c).

Similarly, St John Damascene:

> The benefits of Mary are not limited to one place (pilgrimages to her tomb). Few then would be the beneficiaries of these divine gifts. But in all parts of the world, she generously shares herself. Let us dispose our memories to take a trip with the Virgin. How will that be done? ... She flies from every vice and rejoices at every virtue ... If, therefore, we resolutely combat vice, if we cultivate the virtues with great zeal and get our companions to do likewise, Mary will come often to visit her faithful servants, bringing with her everything that is good, in company with Christ, her Son, King and Master of all, who remains in our hearts (Sermon 2 *On the Dormition*, no. 19, p. 96, 752 bc).

And again:

> Does not the very precious grace of always having your

> memory present to the mind contain everything in itself? (Sermon 1 *On the Assumption*, p. 96, 721 ab)

The same experience of her presence appears during the Middle Ages, starting with the eleventh century.

'Sweet is her memory but sweeter is her presence', the author of the *Liber Salutatorius* wrote (undoubtedly *St Peter Damian*, edited by J. Leclercq, *Ephemerides Liturgicae*, 72, 1958, *p* 303).

Odo of Morimond, who died in 1161, invites us always to have Mary present before our eyes, like John, to whom Mary was entrusted at the foot of the Cross.

> Following the example of the disciple, let us be the disciples whom you loved as you stood (close to the Cross), so that each of us may have the joy of hearing from Jesus these tender words:
> — This is your Mother (*John 19:24*).
> O worthy word of our welcome! Behold your Mother, love her and venerate her, as everywhere present to you. Don't expect anything more. But at that hour, receive her into your own home, in order that she may take you into glory, where she reigns with her Son, who is above all: Blessed be God for ever and ever. Amen!

And St Anthony of Padua (1195-1231), Doctor of the Church, whose canonisation broke all records, taking place less than two years after his death, concluded one of his principal homilies with this prayer:

> We beseech you, Our Lady, our hope, tossed about as we are by the storm. You, Star of the sea, bright ray, direct us towards safe harbour, assist our arrival by the protection of your presence (*Tuae Presentiae Tutela*: Sermon 3 in *Praise of the Virgin* (*Op.* 1, p. 163, 3-7).

In the seventeenth century, references to Mary are more psychological. They disclose spiritual experiences: 'every time that I enter into a place consecrated to this august queen, I feel, with a certain sense of trepidation, that I am in the house of my Mother', St Francis de Sales declared. This was cited by Fr Vincent (*In Maria* 2, pp. 994-995). 'Our Lady is present to Christians by attention', he stated further in a sermon on the angelic salutation.

Similarly, Jean Jacques Olier (1608-1657):

> One Saturday, Mary became interiorally present to my soul... She recalled to me that her dear son had told me that he would only live in me through her and in her and from the life he was living in her, as if she were a sacrament by which he wished to communicate his life to me. (Brettonvillers, *L'esprit de Monsieur Olier*, t. 1, 1, 9, pp. 396-397).

These are only samples from a dossier on this presence of Mary, gathered together over thirty years, which will have to be edited some day. In the seventeenth century the theme becomes commonplace. A work was specifically devoted to it: the *Treatise on the Marylike Life* of Miguel of St Augustine who died in 1684. In this work, he describes the spiritual experience of the Flemish woman, Marie of Saint Thérèse (Marie Petyt: 1623-1677), to whom he gave spiritual direction.

The most intense moments from the experience of this Carmelite tertiary have been retained. But if we look at it closely it proceeds from the deepening of an ordinary devotion to some apparitions with the gift of infused presence, and then *to an eclipse of this sense of the presence* of Mary, for the sake of attaining Christ alone and God alone, who, from the beginning, penetrated and animated everything else. Thus she explains quite well that this presence of Mary is not an obstacle to the presence of Christ even if, at certain moments, it is especially fruitful.

> There is not, in this case, the least obstacle or screen interposed, between the pure being of God and the soul. There is instead assistance furnished to the soul, allowing it to come more easily to God and to become more perfectly rooted in him .... Filial love toward Mary does not cause any difficulty for the divine life of God .... The Spirit of God acts at the appropriate time, without making adherence to and union with God more immediate, but in such a way that it finds, on the contrary, nourishment and a firmer foundation for divine and godlike life (*Mystical Union with Mary*, 1936, p. 61).

We find this lively experience not only in the case of Mary of the Incarnation but also in Marie-Claire Arnaud of Port Royal, for whom Mary is, as she once wrote, 'the sole way by which I can hope for God's mercy'. She observed further:

> The majority of the time I am totally occupied with her and only live under her shadow (letter to Monsieur Singlin in *Mémoire pour servir à l'histoire de Port Royal*, Utrecht, 1942, t. 3, p. 471).

This presence shines forth throughout the writings of Grignion de Montfort, often expressed poetically:

> She is my divine oratory
> where I always find Jesus
> I pray there with glory
> (Canticle 77, strophe 6).

and (strophe 15, even more striking):

> Here is what we can believe:
> I carry her right in the midst of me,
> engraved with traits of glory,
> although in the obscurity of faith.

Let us not pick any further from the petals of this dossier which stretches over the centuries and which seems to justify de Montfort's prediction in his *Treatise on True Devotion* (no. 46):

> At the end of the world, the greatest saints will be those who are most devoted to praying to the most Holy Virgin, and who *have had her always present*, as their perfect model, in order to imitate her and to have her as their powerful helper in *their time of need.*

5. So many children, so much love

Mary's presence is certainly a fact. But so many children! some will say. Such a multitude can only scatter and reduce love. This objection is quite similar to the question that the mother of an only son posed to the mother of a large family, reported at an international conference on the family, in Paris in September 1986: 'But how can you love so many children? I have great difficulty in loving only one!' 'But for me each child is unique', she responded. 'For each child my heart grows larger.'

The heart of Mary grows larger, as we have said, not only to the extent with which nature abundantly endows mothers of large families but to the measure of God whose life she shares. For Mary, each one of us is unique. She loves us all together and the universality of her love intensifies the love of each in Jesus Christ.

This presence is strong on Mary's part; on our part, she is not appreciated and it is up to us to find how to actualise her place in our life: what image, what sign (maybe a scapular or medal), what prayer or practice, pilgrimages or promises? I prefer to leave the choice up to each person as it is more desirable that each person's filial love find its own forms and modes of expression, its bonds, since every filial bond is personal.

In actualising this unappreciated presence, we allow our mother to help us better for she does not act like an intruder; she does not do anything without us but with us.

Characteristics of this presence

Those who have attempted to discover her presence have sometimes come to enjoy a presence which is habitual, ardent, purifying and peaceful.

> It is a gift of the habitual presence of the Holy Virgin, as it is a gift of the habitual presence to God, very rare, it is true, leading however to very great fidelity (Chaminade, *The Spirit of our Foundation*, Vol 1, p. 173).

This does not mean a visible presence. Louis Cestac (1801-1868), whose life was so strikingly filled with this presence, once answered those who questioned him:

> No, I do not see her, but I sense her, as the horse senses the hand of the person who rides him (text quoted by P. Bordarrampe, *The Venerable L. E. Cestac*, Paris, Gigord, 1925, p. 458).

Once again, this presence is only the proper recognition (the attentive, continuous recognition) of the real presence of Mary in the communion of saints.

Let us attempt to characterise this presence and the ways and means of cultivating it.

A presence in God and for God

1 It is a presence different from that of God.

The presence of God is transcendent. He is our creator: he brought us into being. He is the permanent principle of our existence. If he ceases to wish it (which is not thinkable, since God is constant and faithful), we cease to exist, as the light goes out when the current no longer passes through the wires. He is then more intimately linked to our being than we are to ourselves.

This creative presence does not overwhelm us since it gives rise to autonomy and liberty: a marvellous yet unappreciated mystery. I dream about a psychoanalysis which would no longer be concerned with the impulses of our lowest depths but with this fundamental presence, which gives meaning, order and fulfilment to all the rest.

The presence of Mary is not on this level for she is a creature like us. The world existed before she existed. If she ceases to think of us we will not cease to exist. It is not she who brought us into being. Created by God, she only knew how to cooperate with God for our well-being.

2 The presence of God is not only the presence of the creator, it also establishes the order of grace, by which he communicates his very life to us. This presence is much more radical than a decadent theology used to describe it: grace (actual or even habitual) was presented here as 'something': a sort of object, deposited by God into the soul, which Mary, according to the usual understanding of mediation, would be capable of transmitting. During the time of Pius XII the Holy Office reacted properly in order to exclude a definition of universal mediation which would have run the risk of lessening and disfiguring grace.

For grace is the very life of God communicated to us, according to *John 7:38-39 (cf 4, 10, 14),* where grace, that is the Holy Spirit himself, wells up in us as source of living water, in accordance with Christ's desire: 'That they may have life and have it to the full' (*John 10:10*). Grace is therefore the immediate actualisation of our soul (of our being) by God. He communicates his very life to us, his transcendent love. He makes us divine, in accordance with love, without changing our nature in any way. Mary's presence is not of this order. It is not, like the Father, the Son and the Holy Spirit, the divine principle of grace, the source of life, for she herself receives divine life from God; she is not the author of the new creation but the servant of the Lord.

Result: the presence of Mary is a presence *in* God and *by* God. And it is certainly in this way that the mystics perceive it as being as inseparable from God as the stream is from its source. It is a presence which emanates from the Father, a presence in Christ, in his body which is the Church, a presence in the Holy Spirit, the bond of the Trinity and of the Church, through this life of love which he infuses.

A permanent presence in faith

3 It is not a presence of feeling, even if it is good to have a feeling about it. It is a presence in faith: a consciousness of our bonds with Mary, in Christ and the communion of saints, according to revelation itself.

4 It is a permanent universal presence, as we have seen, like her presence in scripture and the liturgy.

A feminine and maternal presence

5 It is a human and feminine presence.

— *Human*, like that of Christ, who is thus so near and so intimate to us.
— *Feminine*, which is proper to her. She is the summit of the admirable and unappreciated mission given to women by God: closer to life than men who are distanced from it because of the desire to master and govern it from outside.

6 It is a maternal presence: Mary, Mother of Christ, universal man because he is God-man, has unfolded an integral motherhood: integrally referred to God, but also integrally and universally human, in accordance with the vocation with which she was conferred from the Cross when he said: 'Woman, this is your son' (*John 13:27*).

What adoption means

This new maternity is adoptive. But the adoption is not a reduced motherhood. It is a bilateral adventure of reciprocity. For the adoptive mother it is certainly no small thing to be accepted by the adopted child and to adopt him!

I knew a childless woman who decided, with her husband, upon an adoption. The child in question was nearly a year old. She made several visits to him so that he might become accustomed to her. But he always looked at the nurse who was responsible for him. The adoptive mother was very troubled by this invincible barrier. Her husband tried to calm her down: 'For you, this is more important than our engagement!' The analogy was significant.

One stormy day, there was a particularly loud clap of thunder. The child was afraid. This time he sought refuge in the arms of his visitor. She had become his mother. It was a decisive moment in her life.

Another mother of a (remarkable) family, who already had several children, adopted a Vietnamese orphan out of Christian and human concern. This was difficult. The child remained a stranger. He was already four or five years old and only spoke his mother tongue, not one word of French. He would hide, disappear. She went looking for a Vietnamese family so that he might be able to play, speak and feel at ease. She was looking for an harmonious environment in which he would rediscover the roots that she was unable to give to him. But when she brought him to this ideal family, the child did not speak and only played for a short period. He came to her, seeking refuge at her knees, and would not let go of her. Fear over the prospect of a further move overcame him and he would not have left his mother for an empire. Unknown to her, she had already become his mother. She took him home and there was no longer any distance between them.

No, adoption is not a reduced motherhood. Motherhood endures. It is woven of a fabric which goes beyond genetics in a responsible, indestructible and attentive manner. Mary lived out the most universal and profound experience of this: by learning first of all to be Mother of God, and then, with a very sad surprise, mother of sinful humanity.

Mary's motherhood for us is thus a spiritual, moral, existential motherhood accomplished in the divine order, and it is a real motherhood since an adoptive mother is a true mother and not an unnatural or alien mother.

It seems artificial, after that, to consider when and how Mary would have begotten us. Certainly we can say, with Revelation, that Mary suffered the pangs of childbirth on Calvary. This image has a very profound sense but does not authorise us to search for the mechanics of a particular type of childbirth which would be in accordance with a biological model.

Nothing possessive in Mary

Let us be even more specific. In order to take issue with some deceitful images, Mary is not a possessive mother. The artificial model of an overly sensitive mother, who is nosy, manipulative and uses mental blackmail: 'You don't love me any more, so much the worse for you!', has sometimes been projected upon her.

In Jesus' case, Mary was not a possessive mother. She allowed him to go along in the caravan without keeping an eye on him. She waited a whole day before setting out to look for him (*Luke 2:40-46*). Likewise, she respects the liberty of her adopted children. Her demands are not blackmail, but an invitation to perceive God and Christ alone as capable of filling us to overflowing. As marvellous, as perfect as this motherhood of Mary might be, let us avoid personalising it by means of the deceptive presuppositions of too many theologians.

It is not proper to reduce Mary to her condition as mother, important as this may be. She is not the essence (in the Platonic sense) of motherhood. She is a human person. She exists with all the liberty and freedom of choice which this involves. And the Holy Spirit stimulates in her not only the exercise of her maternal duties but also, from a reasonable distance, respectful of others, he also stimulates creativity, this imagination which flourishes in liberty. Her concern reflects that of the Holy Spirit who inspires her transparently: to arouse each of her children, each community, each Church to better themselves, according to their diversity and their own proper vocation.

7 It is a discreet presence, because everything is referred to Christ, to God, as the dynamic episodes of the Visitation and Cana illustrate: 'Do whatever he tells you' (*John 2:4*). Several mystics have noted that after manifesting herself, at times intensely, Mary knows how to disappear in order to lead us to Christ alone. It is good to follow her interior orientations.

How to cultivate this presence

How to make it a reality

We can cultivate this presence by actualising the signs which are given to us in the life of the Church:

- scripture itself, as we have seen;
- the liturgy: Mary is present in each Mass, and throughout the entire year, sanctoral and temporal;
- churches, sanctuaries and pilgrimages which are dedicated to her;
- images which are signs of her presence: an image is not an object under glass. It is a window opened upon the communion of saints. It is a glance, a look;
- devotions: among which we may have a choice. Paul VI especially recommended the Angelus and the Rosary.

We can profitably confide our projects and our undertakings to Mary in order not to remove ourselves from them but to have better control over them with her, through faith, in God. What is entrusted to her is not lost.

It is important above all to know how to welcome the gift of this presence as it is given, whether it takes place in a lively or dull fashion. This unconditional gift must not be the object of impatience or of disturbance. Its occasional vivacity will only last for a time. Thérèse of Lisieux recounts how she lived, for eight days, 'hidden under the mantle of our Lady, doing things as though not doing them'. But this valuable onrush of our Lady's presence would only last eight days, quite a short time, in relation to a life which would be filled with all types of trials over a long period of time. This was a productive stage, not a definitive Tabor. It is important to grasp this presence in order to live it:

— as a child of Mary, without being infantile;
— as a servant, without servility;
— as a son, without passive dependence;
— as a brother of this older sister in admiration of the exemplary prototypical and foundational grace which she had so wonderfully taken upon herself.

We should not be overly focused upon this gift, or wait to see progress being made, since the actualisation of the presence of Mary usually includes strong as well as weak periods. And it is inappropriate to act at the wrong moment or to become disturbed by a return to a state of total reserve.

Since these 'strong' times bear fruit, it can be useful to discern them and to know when they are given.

The strong times

The strong times in our life reflect what they are in scripture, liturgy, the life of the Church and the experience of the saints:

1 *Mary is the Virgin of beginnings*: She has played an initiating and foundational role: in the Incarnation and the infancy of Christ; at Cana, the inaugural sign of the ministry of Jesus; then in the infancy of the Church, born on Pentecost.

She will also be the Virgin of beginnings for us. It is good to entrust to her whatever we are undertaking, whatever the Lord inspires us to do so that she will help us to see it through. It is the custom of many mothers to offer their child to Mary as soon as they are aware of the child's existence. She who, to the greatest extent, realised the beginning has the mission to help us in our beginnings to lead them to their conclusion.

2 *Mary is the Virgin of transitions* (this is the same thing since there is no beginning without transition and beginnings themselves are transitions). The Annunciation is the beginning of the New Testament but it is also a passage from the old to the new. At Cana, the 'first sign' which the initiative of Mary obtained precipitated the transition from the hidden to the public life. Let us entrust to Mary these transitions, crises, delicate and difficult moments of our lives as well as our projects and our ministries.

3 *She is the Virgin of spiritual nights*: 'Star of the Sea', as she has been called since the middle ages, our Lady of the *Stabat*, the tragic icon of Golgotha. She plays a significant role in the sorrowful transitions, the trials and the crosses. In times of desolation and darkness, she does not suppress death and darkness, she herself did not escape them, she learns to live these experiences out in faith. She procures peace from the Cross and at night. Let us think of her, when we are overwhelmed by events, by internal difficulties, by sickness, or 'at the hour of our death', as we pray in the Hail Mary. She has a vocation to come to our assistance, after our daily trials, in this ultimate trial of life. She is our mother at the hour of our birth in heaven.

Mary's presence is free and varied. Let us know how to welcome it in the freedom of the children of God.

2. CONSECRATION

We spoke first of the presence of Mary: a vital, traditional theme which, in a profound and indisputable fashion, expresses the essence of our relationship to God. This is why this formula seems to be preferable to those which are apparently stronger and more captivating, but which are, in fact, more ambiguous, such as mediation, coredemption or even Mother of the Church: even though 'presence' does not say it all, and other formulas are also legitimate.

Another word has assumed a major place in the marian literature of recent centuries: consecration.

The remarkable increase in the so-called marian consecrations

Having some antecedents in the Middle Ages, these consecrations, strictly linked to Mary, became a spiritual movement in Spain in the sixteenth and seventeenth centuries and were then brought further afield by Grignion de Montfort and many others. Since the Second World War, three popes, on eight occasions, renewed the consecration of the world to the Immaculate Heart of Mary with great urgency. This was in response to the request of Lucy, the visionary of Fatima. Mary holds one of the foremost places in the Christian enterprise of consecration.

Some serious theological objections

However, this generous fervour has given rise to reservation and even polemic. We speak a great deal of consecration to Mary. She consecrates us, one is consecrated. Theologians pose the following serious objections to this language:

1 God alone consecrates.
2 Consecration is baptism.
3 How can one consecrate *oneself* since it is God who consecrates?
4 How can others be consecrated, atheistic Russia, for example, since a consecration cannot exist without the personal and free agreement of the one whom God is consecrating?
5 One can only be consecrated to God.

'What do your consecrations signify?' a famous theologian wrote to me. 'You consecrate yourself, you consecrate others. I do not understand. God alone consecrates, that is to say takes possession of us and divinises our being and our life'.

This is true and we ought not to forget it: every consecration is an unconditional gift of God, which begins through him and ends with him, for only he can conquer the inertia of our secular nature and lift us up to his divine life (*cf John 10:35:* you are gods...).

John Paul II did not ignore this objection. He took it up and resolved it by referring to the words of Jesus at the Last Supper.

> I consecrate myself so that they too may be consecrated (*John 17:19*).

This text recalls to us that there is only one consecration: that of Jesus Christ. By being born among men, he has consecrated his humanity through the anointing of his very divinity, and this consecration, internal to the created world, is a principle of consecration for the entire world: radically consecrated by him, called to enter into his consecration. Both our destiny and that of the world is consecration in Jesus Christ, communicated and diffused throughout the world.

7 The second objection, that there is only one consecration, baptism, is as legitimate as the first. Through this sacrament, God consecrates us, impressing upon us an indelible character.

Perhaps speaking of other consecrations would obscure the consecration of baptism and bog us down in minute detail? It would not, for these votive consecrations have a well-established role in the tradition of the Church, notably religious consecration by the three vows.

The word consecration being analogous, this 'religious consecration' is relative. It has no other purpose than to realise effectively the consecration of baptism. Likewise, the consecrations to Mary or by Mary. Christian preaching and Grignion de Montfort himself did not cease to stress this point with the greatest clarity. To be consecrated is to open oneself actively and generously to the consecration of God.

These actualisations or votive consecrations are no less important and it is a tragedy in the Church that many baptisms are baptisms of still-born infants. God has done his work of consecration but without any response on the part of the baptised: a fundamental consecration has not passed into a person's life.

The chief element of our destiny and of the Church itself is, therefore, that this consecration, freely given by God, should obtain a response. From a seed it should become a living plant, from a promise it should become productive; it should penetrate our entire life; our being should be purified, baptised, oriented towards God, should move towards God, the life of God should enter into all zones, even the most secret of our being, and into all the acts of our life in order to transfigure them. According to theology (and the great preachers of the seventeenth century such as Bourdaloue), this is the meaning of religious consecration through the three vows of poverty, chastity and obedience. Its purpose is to actualise, to realise the consecration of baptism.

This is also the function of some consecrations through Mary.

I say *some* consecrations for they can take various forms: that of de Montfort, to Jesus through Mary, which was requested at Fatima through the Immaculate Heart of Mary and so on.

To speak of consecration it is, therefore, important to speak of God, that is to say, of the Holy Spirit. Baptism in the Spirit is nothing other than the living actualisation of sacramental baptism and its penetration into the hidden zones of our being, even into the unconscious.

This sets the stage for allowing us to resolve a third objection:

3 Since only God consecrates, why speak of consecrating oneself?

It is because God does nothing in us without us. He can only consecrate us upon our request with our acceptance and our cooperation. Certainly, God does all (as primary creative cause), but he summons us to do everything with him on our level, as free and necessary secondary cause. The work of our consecration, given entirely by him, is accomplished through us: through our freedom.

It is certainly true that the word *consecrate* does not have the same meaning when we say that God *consecrates us*, that is to say transforms us, and when we speak of *consecrating ourselves*, that is to say: accepting and living out fervently this grace of God. This cooperation is important and necessary.

4 But can others be consecrated since they are unable to be consecrated without their free consent? Isn't consecrating Russia, (according to the request from Fatima) an officially atheist state, a whimisical proposal and an attack upon the liberty of other people, a violation, indeed, of the rights of man? We will return later to the meaning of these votive consecrations, inspired by a desire to obtain, for some third parties or groups, the best of gifts: God. It is clear that this gift cannot be obtained without the liberty of those involved. These consecrations seek to help those, in these countries, who already are consecrated, in spite of all their trials and persecutions, in order that the light and the gift that they are living be extended to their compatriots who are plunged into the darkness and the shadow of death. It is therefore a prayer, an intercession, an appeal to the generous gift of Christ, who consecrated himself in order to consecrate humankind with him. He is not prohibited from swooping down upon atheistic countries, as he did in the case of St Paul, the persecutor, in order to consecrate him, in this marvellous

manner, for the apostolate which became the joy and the ardent purpose of his life.

5 What follows is the objection which has the greatest relevance to our subject: why do we speak of consecration to Mary? We can only be consecrated to God.

The objection is well founded. Consecration bespeaks total commitment and, paradoxically, the formula of consecration sometimes accentuates the totalitarianism of this giving of self by stating: 'I consecrate myself as a slave'. The formula is shocking since slavery is evil. To make a slave of a creature (to be consecrated to a creature) would be an alienation, a reduction to a state of bondage, a disregard for the rights of man and for human autonomy.

But the objection can be overcome if a person is consecrated to God, like the apostle Paul, who described himself, with such great insistence, as a slave of Christ (*Romans 1:1*, and the prologue to numerous epistles).

It is overcome since God is creator and consecrating oneself to him is not to alienate oneself, it is to recognise a truth: our condition as creature, a condition in which we owe everything entirely to God including our existence and our very freedom, which he creates as a freedom which is capable of turning away from him and from the good. To accept this truth is to discover, at the same time, both the beginning and the divine end of our existence. It is to discover the deepest reality and the very source of our liberty so often enslaved by illusions here below. It is to find the way to the sole happiness, which counts in this world and leads to eternity and for eternity: happiness which grafts us on to the plenitude of love.

This perspective can seem peculiar for those of us who are involved in the vicissitudes of this world, leading our lives like fleeting animals, up to the point of the final and inevitable catastrophe of death.

The creator calls us to something else. He calls us in accordance with the freedom which he has given us. It is really a freedom in which everyone can do whatever they wish, including turning against God and involving themselves in the frenzy of all sorts of sins.

But freedom was not created for this self-destruction. It was created so that goodness, love and happiness could be discovered, and all of these gifts can only be discovered definitively in God, and in everything which is in God.

We are made to discover happiness through our perfect consecration to God. It is in relation to these fundamental truths that we can locate the role of Mary in these consecrations. If it is relative in its relation to God, it is nonetheless important, since God himself has given her an unequalled place.

3. THE ROLE OF MARY IN THE CONSECRATION

1. *Model in various stages*

First of all, Mary is the *model* of consecration. She is the most perfectly consecrated of redeemed creatures.

1 She has been consecrated, from the beginning, by God, who preserved her from all sin and took possession of her before the awakening of her conscience and freedom but without diminishing her self-awareness. It is in fact, quite the opposite. This freely-made first gift of Mary is analogous to that of baptism.

In the thanksgiving expressed in the Magnificat, Mary's freedom has not ceased to ratify this consecration of her entire soul unreservedly.

> My spirit rejoices in God my Saviour,
> because he has looked upon the humiliation of his servant.
> Yes, from now onwards all generations will call me blessed,
> for the Almighty has done great things for me.

2 This consecration received a new, and deeper meaning, when Mary became Mother of God at the Annunciation. This personal relationship with the Son of God, and even with the entire Trinity, calls for a new gift of the Holy Spirit: *The Holy Spirit* will *come upon you* (*Luke 1:35*). This is done not only to give human existence to the Son of God but to adapt Mary to this divine relationship, since God added a new relationship, maternal, to her filial relationship with him. This does not destroy the preceding relationship but deepens and transfigures it. We could be tempted to speak of a transmutation which adapts Mary to this unexpected relationship and makes her a worthy Mother of God. This is also her royal dimension, described in terms of a biblical custom in which the queen was not one of the king's spouses, not even the first, but was, rather, the mother of the

one who reigned. It is to her that the monarch granted the throne, diadem and honours. Bathsheba prostrated herself before her spouse David, but it is her son, King Solomon, who prostrated himself before her and had her sit on a throne beside that from which he reigned.

3 At Calvary, a new deepening of Mary's consecration takes place: this is her trial, because the human death of her son has destroyed her motherhood. Motherhood is a relationship and a relationship is defined by two boundaries: in this case, son and mother. When one of these boundaries disappears (the son who dies), the relationship disappears, in a shattering fashion, and in this way, every mother experiences the death of her son, even if she seeks beyond the grave to maintain a relationship with him. On Calvary, Mary accepted a deadly void and Jesus invited her to fill that void through adoption.

Mary's new mission requires a new consecration, which the Lord gave her for this new purpose. It matters little if you prefer to call it a new deepening of the same consecration: of mother and servant of the Lord.

This profound consecration is linked to that of Christ the Redeemer, it is correlative. Mary underwent a thousand deaths in her motherhood, through the death of her son who himself accepted his own death. She endured this at the foot of the Cross where she was on the verge of collapsing.

The trial of Calvary constitutes one stage for both of them. Mary had acquired her vocation as mother of the members of the mystical body by becoming mother of the head through the Incarnation. At that moment, he was still the head, she was still mother of men only by vocation. It was on Calvary that Jesus effectively became our chief and head, by the victory of the Redemption and correlatively, Mary became mother through the sorrowful childbirth on Calvary. Jesus and Mary then became fully, effectively and correlatively what they were by vocation from the beginning.

4 At Pentecost, the Holy Spirit came upon the Church but also upon Mary, for a new spiritual anointing which made her the living and praying heart of his Church: her role was fulfilled. She was, from the beginning, the initial and germinal cell, the matrix of the Holy Church through her prayer, her godly life, her communion with Christ. The Spirit established his organic

bonds with the infant Church wherein the same grace is being extended.

5 At the Assumption, this consecration is unveiled and is accomplished in glory. This is the final stage in which Mary discovers, through the beatific vision, communion with all her children.

Every consecration is from God. But it is also a long march: the first glow of the joyful mysteries to the glorious mysteries through the sorrowful mysteries. Such was the case with Mary.

She is, therefore, the model of perfect consecration, by her continuous movement towards God, by her free acceptance of the gift of God, and by her thanksgiving for this gift. In this, she is a model of the Church, as she is also by her communion with Christ, her godly life and her charisms. The Church is carried along in the wake of her love.

Cooperator with God in the consecration of Christ

But this is not all. Mary plays an active and foundational role in the consecration of Christ himself: the Incarnation. He receives from her this human life which he consecrates by accepting it. Entering into the world this way (*Hebrews 10:5*), he consecrates the world, 'I consecrate myself so that they too may be consecrated' (*John 17:19*).

The consecration of Christ is the work of God alone, of the son assuming this human existence which is born through Mary. But Mary gives to the Son of God this human life, in which he also becomes her son: a single son of the Father and the mother, in accordance with an unalterable sonship. She has furnished the Son of God with the living matter of his consecration, as priest and as victim, since it is through this humanity that he becomes priest and victim and, as such, is consecrated. In this he is the model of our consecration.

The human face of the admirable exchange

In this covenant between God and humanity, Mary has been the indispensable means. She has realised the human part of the admirable exchange between God and us. Like every mother, she has given to the God-made-man not only his body, but also the human awakening and dynamism through which he realised the effective consecration of his humanity during the period of his growth. For he cooperated, humanly, with his consecration: in person he is divine, incarnated in this humanity.

The divine face
God's gifts being irrevocable, the Lord exercised vigilance so that the other face of this exchange might be accomplished in Mary: the humanisation of God and the divinisation of man taking place, first of all, in her. For this work of salvation, the mother of the God-man had to be co-natural with him, not only on the human plane, but by grace, on the divine plane.

Thus she was passionately and totally engaged in this divine-human adventure in which she was the first agent. Nothing that followed, nothing which flowed forth from it, is foreign to her. She remains present everywhere in the admirable exchange which continues. This is what we mean when we speak of universal mediation. Nothing is foreign to her in this symbiosis of God and of man which is definitely consecration. She remains the model, the initiator, the helper of the Church, like an older sister who has become our mother.

4. MARY'S MOTHERLY ASSISTANCE

This is why Jesus established Mary as mother of humanity at the hour that she lost him.

On that occasion Mary adopted us totally and lovingly. Since she has shared the life of God, his love and his knowledge, she knows us, she loves each of us personally by virtue of this knowledge. She awakens in us the love of God, she helps us by the power of her son which she shares. She contributes to the formation of our chrysalis, ready to hatch in heaven. For her this is the grace of being mother, it is her way of spending her heaven doing good upon earth, just as Thérèse of Lisieux hoped to do.

If we can only, in this proper sense, be consecrated to God, it is worth entrusting ourselves to Mary for that purpose. Whoever is entrusted to this very loving mother, beloved of God, is not lost and those who have done so have never been disappointed.

This is what is murmured in the ancient Christian prayer still recited in many households, even though it has disappeared from the majority of Churches.

> Remember, O most loving Virgin Mary, that never was it known, that anyone who ever had recourse to your protection,

implored your help, or sought your intercession, was left forsaken. Filled therefore with confidence in your goodness I fly to you, O Mother, Virgin of virgins. To you I come, before you I stand, sinful and sorrowful. Despise not my poor words, O Mother of the Word Incarnate, but graciously hear and grant my prayers.

The urgency of consecrating a secularised world

During this year with Mary, the experience of this consecration should start with each one of us and be extended to the entire world. In this way, the real tragedy of our world will be resolved: the tragedy from which all the others derive. This world is fundamentally consecrated through the Incarnation of the Son of God and the Redemption of Jesus Christ, but it is not effectively consecrated. It is, to a great extent, opposed to God (atheistic), foreign to God (agnosticism is increasing more quickly than atheism) or, what is still worse, indifferent to God, lukewarm to God. It is the lukewarm which Christ says he will vomit from his mouth (*Revelation 3:16*).

Will the Pope renew the consecration of Russia during this year with Mary? Many are asking him to do so on the occasion of the millenium of Christianity in that country. But it is up to him to decide. This effective consecration will only be realised at the culmination of a consecration of the entire world, as Pius XII perceived by broadening the request of Lucy of Fatima. Are we confident that Mary will put an end to our apathy and lead us to a perfect consecration of love to God who loves us, to Christ her son, with whom she shares everything? It is to this that she invites us:

Do whatever he tells you (*John 2:5-6*).

The Holy Spirit, agent and anointing of every consecration

If we want to get to the root of this divine and human movement of the consecration of Christ, Mary and ourselves, if we wish to understand its unity, we must return to the Holy Spirit, to the principle of all these consecrations. It is in him that the coherence of this divine anointing, of his dynamism, of his inspiration, is understood.

One of the great secrets to be discovered during the year with Mary are these exemplary bonds with the Holy Spirit. In the Scriptures, from the Annunciation to Pentecost, Mary always appears in the company of the Holy Spirit and he, likewise, more discreetly, is with her at Cana and on Calvary. The invisible spirit is bound to the visible woman who has made God visible. He invested himself in her and she gave herself up to the Spirit. Wherever Mary is, he hurries to, as Mary hurries to wherever the Spirit blows: from Nazareth to Cana and to Pentecost. She is pure transparency, pure manifestation of the Holy Spirit against whom we erect so many barriers. It is with him that Mary is present to us and helps us to realise our consecration to God alone, with the fullness of love in all its hundredfolds, the wonders of which she knows so very well.

5. PRAYER WITH MARY, BY MARY, TO MARY

Prayer to Mary is not the summit of the prayer of the Church. As we have seen, she is only a secondary and derivative aspect.

The visionaries of Medjugorje understand this well. For them, the high point of each apparition is not the moment when they speak with Mary but the moment when they pray *with* her.

What follows are some cxamples of the various forms of the prayer listed above.

With Mary

For prayer with Mary, the most ancient and superb prototype is the opening of the first *anaphora* (fourth century) just before the Consecration of the Mass.

Communicantes et memoriam venerantes in primis Beatae Mariae...

> United in communion (with all the Church), we celebrate in the first place the Blessed Mary ever Virgin, Mother of our God and Lord Jesus Christ.

By Mary

Under this ambiguous title are listed some examples of Mary's place in the basic prayer of the Church addressed to 'the Father through Christ'.

She has a beautiful place in the prayer of Christmas, as well as in the prayers of personal feasts.

1 She can be an *incentive* for the prayer addressed to the Father, as in the prayer for the feast of the Visitation:

All powerful God, you have inspired the Virgin Mary, carrying within her your own Son, to visit her cousin Elizabeth. Grant that we be open to the inspiration of the Spirit, in order that we may also be able to glorify you eternally through Jesus Christ our Lord.

Mary appears at the same time both as a *model* and as an *incentive* for prayer.

2 Other prayers depend upon her intercession. Likewise the prayers of the saints depend upon her for their example and their intercession.

Prayer to Mary

Prayer addressed to Mary may be a more recent, less ancient, more intimate and less official form of prayer.

As we have seen, it started quite early. In the east from the third or fourth century; in the west in the fifth century. She also has her place in the lyric parts of the Mass, the hymns, such as the *Stabat Mater*, for the feast of the Sorrows of Mary on the fifteenth of September, in which certain strophes are addressed to her:

O sweet Mother! font of love,
Through my spirit from above,
Make my heart with yours accord.

Make me feel as you have felt:
Make my soul to glow and melt
  With the love of Christ, my Lord.

Holy Mother, pierce me through,
In my heart each wound renew
  Of my Saviour crucified.

Let me share with you his pain,
Who for all our sins was slain,
  Who for me in torments died.

Let me mingle tears with you,
Mourning him who mourned for me,
  All the days that I may live.

By the cross with you to stay,
There with you to weep and pray,
  Is all I ask of you to give.

But this hymn concludes with the prayer to her Son and not to her:

Christ, when you shall call me hence,
Be your Mother my defence,
  Be your cross my victory.

While my body here decays,
May my soul your goodness praise,
  Safe in heaven eternally.
Amen. (Alleluia)

The Introits of certain of her Masses address themselves to Mary, notably the following taken from *Judith 13:23,25*:

You are blessed, Virgin Mary, by the Most High God
more than all women on the earth;
never may the glory that has been given to you
be removed from the memory of men.
(Third Mass of the Common of the Blessed Virgin)

or again:

Blessed are you, O Virgin Mary:
you have borne the Creator of the universe,
you have brought into the world the very one who made you,
and you remain ever a virgin (Second Mass).

As for private prayers to the Virgin, we have already cited in the main body of the text, the one which is undoubtedly the most ancient: the *Sub tuum;* and the *Memorare*, which is the source of so many conversions and graces.

Among the prayers to Mary, the most distinguished are the Angelus and the Rosary.

1 The Angelus, for a long time so popular, immortalised by the famous painting of Millet (*The angelus*) has been honoured by the Popes who recited it each Sunday with the faithful and recommended it highly. The recitation of the three Hail Marys to celebrate the coming of Christ to Mary began under more limited forms in the twelfth century. Pope Gregory IX, who died in 1241, ordered bells to be rung to promote this prayer on behalf of the Crusades. But it was only in the seventeenth century that the *angelus* received the uniform format with which we are familiar.

2 As for the rosary, although it had many antecedents (various combinations of Paters, Aves and Glorias or other formulas), it was cast in its final form by the Dominican, Alain de la Roche, in 1470, under the title *Psalter of Mary*. With its 150 Aves, it took the place of the Liturgical Office among the illiterate. The 150 Aves recall the number of the Psalms. Alain de la Roche grouped them into fifteen decades for the meditation of the joyful, sorrowful and glorious mysteries. The rosary is a Bible of the poor: so biblical and so evangelical that a Methodist Pastor, Neville Ward, introduced it into his parish, a little before 1970. Before doing so he wrote a little book on the rosary which has been translated into several languages.

6. THE LITURGICAL YEAR WITH MARY

In this table is a summary not only of the feasts, but also of certain other occasions in the temporal cycle in which Mary has her place.

1 January	Holy Mary	6th century	Solemnity
2 February	Presentation of the Lord and the Piercing of Mary (*Luke 2:35*)	7th century	Feast
11 February	Our Lady of Lourdes	1907	Memorial
19 March	St Joseph — Spouse of the Virgin Mary	15th century	Solemnity
25 March	Annunciation of the Lord	7th century	Solemnity
17 April, 1987	Good Friday Passion according to *John 19:25,27*		Solemnity
31 May	The Visitation of the Blessed Virgin Mary	1401	Feast
7 June 1987	Seventh Sunday after Easter Reading from the *Acts of the Apostles 1:14*		
Saturday of the third week after Pentecost	The Immaculate Heart of Mary	1944	Memorial
16 July	Our Lady of Mount Carmel	1726	Memorial
5 August	Dedication of St Mary Major	1570	Memorial
15 August	Assumption	7th century	Solemnity
22 August	The Queenship of Mary	1954	Memorial
8 September	The Nativity of Mary	8th century	Feast

15 September	Our Lady of Sorrows	1814	Memorial
7 October	Our Lady of the Rosary	1573	Memorial
21 November	Presentation of the Blessed Virgin Mary	1371	Memorial
8 December	The Immaculate Conception of Mary	1854	Solemnity
4th Sunday in Advent Year B in 1987	The Gospel of the Annunciation		
Christmas	Mary is an integral part of this feast (The Gospel of the Vigil and of the Masses)	4th century	

This table will help to celebrate the liturgical year with Mary called for by the Pope.

APPENDIX I

A. Notes outside the text — Chapter 1

DISPELLING THE ILLUSIONS WHICH MAKE MARY SO DISTANT

A void

Neglect of Mary is seen today as a void. For about ten years, many Christians have attempted to rediscover her but they have not succeeded very well. The praiseworthy effort to find her in the Bible is compromised by a perspective which relativises the historical truth of the gospel.

Publishers must, of course, concentrate on what might sell well but, unfortunately, many of the essays published on the subject of Mary fluctuate between trendy reductionistic essays and a return to the heavy and specialised vocabulary under which Counter-Reformation mariology sometimes buried Mary.

Causes

The principal causes of this are:

1 A reaction against the excesses (today largely overcome) of pre-conciliar mariology and the marian movement which made of Mary a sign of contradiction not only in other Christian churches but within Catholicism itself.

2 A reductionist exegesis which empties or minimises the historical consistency of Mary and of Christ himself by opposing the Christ of faith (a beautiful mystical construction of the early Christians) to the Christ of history who, in accordance with the techniques of the masters of suspicion, is put through the sieve of negative criticism.

3 Some philosophies, barely compatible with Christianity, which continue to dominate our culture.

- On the one hand, materialism empties the spiritual dimension of Christ and of Mary. We have seen a materialist (Marxist) exegesis in which Mary no longer had any place, flourishing among Catholics.
- On the other hand, the idealism, which still dominates our culture, is taking a much greater toll. Idealism is materialism turned inside out. From this perspective, we are only what we know. The world and history are no longer anything

except a product. Reality is reduced to almost nothing, an unknowable unknown, the 'thing in itself' of Kant's philosophy. In exegesis the Jesus of history is often reduced to this so-called inaccessible state. Christ and Mary are then presented, to varying degrees, as the more or less subjective products of the Christian community. This knowledge, dependent on the spirit (the Holy Spirit, as the more believing fortunately declare), is opposed to the vulgar knowledge of the flesh. This is to forget that the apostles are first of all eye-witnesses: they have seen with their eyes Christ in the flesh: 'Something... which we have seen with our eyes, which we have watched and touched with our own hands, the Word of life' (*1 John 1:1*). It is this very reality which the Holy Spirit has enlightened. The Holy Spirit is not hawking dreams. He has stirred the awareness of this historical reality: the Incarnation. He brings about the realisation that this man among men is God in person. According to reductionist points of view, we can know nothing, or not really that much, about reality and our faith comes from a purely internal, disconnected revelation.

Invent your own Christ. What do you say about him? What do you think about him? This is the approach suggested by a particular type of catechesis which gives insufficient attention to teaching children who Christ is and the importance of encountering him in spirit and in truth. We need to get beyond materialism and idealism (two opposites of one and the same genre) and return to a realist philosophy in which Christian intelligence makes us humble before the reality of the Son of God made man. Unlike those for whom there is more in the gospel than in Christ and more in exegesis than in the gospels, Christian experience knows well that there is more in Christ than in the gospel and more in the gospel than in all our exegeses.

4 Added to all of this has been the influence of rationalism and of sexual liberation which have, consciously or unconsciously, taken the virginity of Mary as their target: an embarrassing model (they would even say repressive) for the unconditional liberation of sacrosanct desire (*libido*).

This is not the place to examine all these factors. In order to know Mary, Mother of the Lord (*Luke 1:42*) we have to free ourselves from all the cultural deformations which reduce or distort her: a difficult intellectual and moral asceticism which prayer often compensates.

It is through prayer that we must begin to rediscover the true knowledge about the Mother of the Lord. After vocal prayer (why not the rosary?) we can ask Christ for his glance (the glance of a child) in order to look at Mary and we can ask Mary for her glance (the glance of a servant, *Luke 1:38* and *48*) in order to look at Jesus being born, dying, risen and glorious.

B. Notes outside the text — Chapter 2

THE MAGNIFICAT, CANTICLE OF MARY

This is not a 'post-resurrectional fabrication which a later Christian community would have officially attributed to Mary'.

All sorts of presuppositions are used in the plot to wrest the Magnificat from Mary. It is said to be a later canticle composed after the Resurrection by some 'community of the poor'.

Such unfounded hypotheses contradict the evidence provided by Luke, who tells us that he is basing himself upon eyewitnesses (*1:2*) such as Mary, who preserved these things in her heart (*Luke 2:19* and *51*). And this canticle is one of her precious memories.

There is nothing 'resurrectional' as has, without any basis, been alleged. In no way is this a matter of the Resurrection.

This canticle was not composed later as is alleged, again without basis. The Jewish exegete, Paul Winter, who is free of these misleading presuppositions, sees instead a Maccabean Psalm, decidely distant in time from Christianity, for nothing in it would have been anachronistic even one or two centuries before Jesus Christ.

This canticle is, moreover, the translation of a canticle into the Semitic language, the retroversion (translation back) of which reveals astonishing allusions to the names of various persons. Mary says:

> My soul rejoices in God my Saviour.

These words echo Habakkuk's phrase (*3:18*), which Jerome translated:

> My spirit exults in God my Jesus.

A legitimate translation, since *Jesus* signifies 'Saviour'. We can translate 'my Saviour' or 'my Jesus' and we can think that Mary actualised, in this latter sense, the word of the angel: 'You must name him Jesus. He will be called Son of the Most High' (*Luke 1:31-32*).

The conclusion of the canticle groups together, in one line, allusions to the names of three other protagonists: Zechariah, John the Baptist and Elizabeth:

> **mindful** (*zachar*, like Zechariah)
> of his **faithful love** (*hanan*: to give thanks or mercy, root of the name John: Yehohanan)
> according to the oath he **swore** (*shabah*: root of the name Elizabeth) to our ancestors.

It is true that the Greek weakens this by using the word *speak* as the translation of this word *swear* which was certainly the Hebrew original: this is the hellenistic elegance of Luke. The proof of this is that this word 'to swear' appears with frequency in a similar passage of the Benedictus (*Luke 1:72-73*) in which the retroversion shows even more clearly the allusion to the names of the same three persons:

> show **faithful love** (the name of John) to our ancestors and so to **keep in mind** (*zachar*, like Zechariah) his holy covenant. This was the **oath** (*shabah*: root of the name Elizabeth) he **swore** (same root which doubles the allusion to the name of Elizabeth) to our father Abraham.

C. Notes outside the text — Chapter 3

DID MARY REMAIN A VIRGIN AFTER CHILDBIRTH?

Did Mary remain a virgin after childbirth?
Mary remained 'ever Virgin'. Her total consecration to God, described with so much depth in *Luke 1:28-38* made the Holy Family an exceptional household. Such has been the belief of Christians for two thousand years. There is no discordant voice up until the time of Helvidius (fourth century) who was quickly put down, and there are isolated cases of this in modern times.

The New Testament does not concern itself with the virginity of Mary after the birth of Christ. Some claim that, in two places, it teaches the opposite.

Up until

The final verse of the first chapter of Matthew (*1:25*) tell us that Joseph did not *know* her ('know' in the sexual sense of this word in the Bible — Adam knew Eve and she gave birth to Cain (*Genesis 4:1, cf 4:25*) — up until she had given birth to a son.

Up until (*eos*)! Therefore Joseph 'knew' her afterwards, as is alleged. But this presupposition signifies only a *limit*, without prejudice to what happens beyond. When *2 Samuel 6:23* says that Michal had no child 'until her death', it is clear that she did not have one afterwards! Mary also would not have had any other after Christ.

The brothers of Jesus

Jesus had brothers and sisters, the gospel states (*Mark 3:31-35; Matthew 13:56*). Since there are brothers, say the critics, let us not play on words, let us recognise them as sons of Mary. But this 'evidence' is deceptive.

1 The word 'brother' had, in biblical Hebrew, a very extended meaning: cousins, uncles, and so on (*Genesis 13:8, 14, 16;29:12* and *15*). References are given in *Court Traité*, p. 176. The Bible preserved this extended meaning in accordance with the Greek Bible usage of the Septuagint.

2 All brothers of the Lord are known by their names: 'James, Joseph, Simon and Jude' (*Matthew 13:55*). James the Less, who is mentioned here, is the son of a Mary who cannot be identified with the Virgin. The latter is generally called the Mother of Jesus (*John 2:1; 19:25; Acts 1:14*); 'the other Mary' is always designated 'the mother of James and of Joseph' (*Mark 15:40; Matthew 27:56*) or 'the mother of Joseph' (*Mark 15:47*), or 'the mother of James' (*16:1*), specifically in order to avoid confusion. This woman is always named after Mary Magdalene.

Not only does the gospel *not* teach that brothers of the Lord are the sons of Mary but it lets us know that two of those who are known by their names are sons of another woman.

Moreover, Hegesippus (author of the second century, quoted by Eusebius in the *Ecclesiastical History* 4, 22, 4) confirms that Simeon (James' successor as Bishop of Jerusalem, perhaps the Simon of *Matthew 13:55*), 'another brother of the Lord', is his 'cousin' (*anepsios*, according to the precise meaning of classical Greek).

The 'brothers of Jesus' constitute a sizeable group. Matthew (*13:55-56*) mentions 'all his sisters'. These have caused a problem in the primitive Church. The first two bishops of Jerusalem (James and Simeon) were 'brothers of the Lord'. Would not this be tantamount to establishing a dynasty? This would hardly be in line with the spirit of the gospel. There were reactions. Mark and John speak, in strict language, of 'brothers of the Lord'. They wanted to seize Jesus. They thought that he had lost his mind (*Mark 3:21*). They despised him (*Mark 6:4*); 'his brothers would not accept him', according to *John 7:5*. And we can imagine the problem that this caused for Mary, who was a hostage of the family clan in which she possessed no authority. But the clan was not homogeneous. After Cana, some 'brothers of Jesus', remained several days with him (*John 2:12*). They are among the founders and pillars of the early community of Jerusalem (*Acts 1:14*). They are recognisable in the Church (*1 Corinthians 9:5;* cf. *Galatians 1:19;* especially Jude (*Mark 6:3*), author of the epistle.

D. Notes outside the text — Chapter 4

THE CONSECRATION OF RUSSIA AND THE HOPE OF ITS CONVERSION

A request, a promise
The consecration of Russia was asked of Lucy by Our Lady of Fatima, 13 June 1929, at Tuy (Spain), as had been the case, she said, since 13 June 1917:

> The moment has come when God is asking the Holy Father, in union with all the bishops of the world, to consecrate Russia to my Immaculate Heart.

In this way, our Lady promised the conversion of Russia.

A diplomatic difficulty
This request met a diplomatic objection. To mention this officially atheistic country by name would have been a provocation. Pius XI (who attempted, in spite of constant failure, to restore the Catholic hierarchy in Russia) did not heed Our Lady's request, but on 31 October 1942, Pius XII responded by consecrating the world:

> especially the 'people separated by error... who profess for you (Mary) a singular devotion and among whom there is not one house which does not honour your true image, today perhaps hidden and preserved for better days.'

At Lucy's request, on 7 July 1952, Pius XII renewed this consecration in a most explicit fashion:

> We confide and consecrate, in a very special way to the Immaculate Heart, the entire Russian people (AAS 44, 1952, p. 511).

Since then, Paul VI (at the Council, on 21 November 1964) and John Paul II have renewed this consecration eight times in all, the last on 24 and 25 March 1984 on the occasion of the closing of the Holy Year.

Since Russia is not yet converted, Lucy seems to think that successive consecrations are insufficient either because Russia has not been explicitly or exclusively named or because the action of the Holy Father has not been accompanied by a simultaneous or collective action of all the bishops of the entire world — hence the campaigns to have this consecration performed again.

If, however, we look at the texts through which Lucy requested this consecration, they show many hesitations and vacillations, which I detailed in my report of September 1986 at the Symposium on Fatima.

An objection of principle

Moreover, some theologians have set forth an objection of principle to such a consecration of Russia: how can people be consecrated without their agreement? How can an officially atheistic people be consecrated against their will? Doesn't the desire to convert them in this way amount to magic?

John Paul II's response

John Paul II responded in great depth to this difficulty by using a text already employed by Christ: 'For their sake I consecrate myself, so that they too may be consecrated in truth' (*John 17:19*). The consecration of the Son of God, incarnate in this world, sacrificed in this world, risen in this world, radically involves the consecration of the entire world.

It involves a mission for the Pope and the bishops, but also for Christians to render this effective by their witness, their preaching, their apostolic action and by devotional consecrations. These actions constitute an intercession which prepares for the effective consecration.

Although the Pope is thinking of the appropriateness of a new consecration of Russia for its millenium (1988), our role as Christians is personally and in solidarity to effect our own consecration.

May we be able to feel solidarity with Russia where so many Christians, many of whom are recent converts among generations educated in atheism, are living out this commitment even though incarcerated in psychiatric hospitals and concentration camps. During this year of grace with Mary the Holy Father is now inviting us to have a sense of solidarity with those whose witness borders on martyrdom.

APPENDIX II

Short commentary on John Paul II's encyclical, *Redemptoris Mater,* on Mary in the life of the pilgrim Church

Towards the year 2000 with the Mother of the Lord and the millennium of Holy Russia

John Paul II's encyclical *Redemptoris Mater*, in its very title, displays a dynamic programme for Mary and the Church. The Church is 'a pilgrim', like Mary, setting out in haste, after the Annunciation, towards the mountains of Judaea (*Luke 1:39*).

The press, which is always concerned with *news*, asked, somewhat embarrassingly, what was new in this encyclical: did it say anything more than the Council (where Mary was referred to more than 100 times); was it intended to be a commentary on what the Council said; and what about the apostolic exhortation of Paul VI, *Marialis Cultus*, which John Paul II quotes and expands upon? The Pope is not proposing new dogmas, or new doctrines, or feasts, in a pre-conciliar fashion. This Pope, whom some consider authoritarian, is not setting forth any master-plan in this particular regard: he is offering a contemplative meditation. He intends to act solely in the interest of spreading the truth.

Is there anything new? The programme of the encyclical is set forth in its very title. The Pope speaks of 'history' (this word appears more than forty times), the 'pilgrimage of Mary and the Church' (more than twenty times), 'route', 'itinerary', 'march'. This vision of time refers less to a philosophy than to Revelation itself, the fervent Christian experience which inspires this text.

This experience harkens back to Karol Wojtyla's youth. Although he lost his mother Emilia, at nine years of age, he had learned from her that Mary is the best of mothers. This discovery was not the result of frustration. He was to make this discovery again some twelve years later, during the war. We have seen (p. 19) how, as a labourer in the compulsory work force in the Solvay factories, he made the 'consecration to Christ through the hands of Mary' according to Grignion de Montfort whom he mentions in the encyclical (par. 45). We also saw how the same consecration was, for Cardinal Wyszynski, the starting point of the 'Polish miracle'. The encyclical does not mention either this experience or any others which would certainly occur to the Pope.

A programme, or dynamic, is defined by its purpose. On this, he is quite clear. He explicitly reveals the motivation which made him decide quite suddenly on this year with Mary: it is a journey, along with her who was chosen to give birth to Christ, towards the third millennium. The second millennium is ending under a pall of sombre and disappointing colours. At the beginning of the century, optimistic scientists put their hope in the infallible progress of science. The world, liberated from God, would thus resolve all its problems; sickness, death and war would be overcome. But our century (the last of the millennium) has seen two world wars and is ending under the threat of a third. It is believed that it can be warded off only by the 'balance of terror', but the arms race has produced an ever-increasing proliferation of atomic, chemical and bacteriological armaments which have started to cause accidents and threaten the life of the world. This is the century in which concentration camps and gulags came into existence: those of Hitler which carried out the genocide of the Jews and many others, in gas chambers and crematoriums, and those of his Marxist adversaries, who added to death what is even more brutal, the destruction of the human soul. We are witnessing a terrible rise in the political blackmail, violence and terrorism which are becoming the hallmarks of our civilisation, as well as economic recession and breakdown in family life which is the result of an inability to enter into a lasting relationship of love. This situation can only change through inspiration from Christ the Saviour and from Mary who was the first to receive this inspiration which the Church continues to hand on.

It is in this spirit that the Pope has proposed the symbolic and significant objective of the year 2000. Christ, physically born of Mary, in the stable at Bethlehem, must be born again in human hearts and communities; Mary holds in safe-keeping the secrets of this future birth.

A secondary purpose moved the Pope to choose the dates 1987-1988:

— 1987 is the sixth centenary of the birth of Christianity in Lithuania (the Pope spoke of this in his announcement of 1 January);
— 1988 is the millennium of Christianity among the people of Russia — 1000 years since the baptism of St Vladimir, Prince of Kiev (Ukraine: par. 50).

What form will this ecumenical programme take? Will the Pope go to Russia as he hopes to do? Will he meet the Patriarch of Moscow? Will he renew the consecration of Russia to our Lady, as Lucy of Fatima hopes? Only the future will tell.

The composition of the encyclical

The Holy Father personally wrote this encyclical in Polish. He submitted the Italian translation (of the draft document) to representatives of a number of Roman congregations or offices (Faith, Christian Unity, Evangelisation) as well as the Roman universities (Marianum, Gregorian) and so on. However, he incorporated only a few suggestions and steadfastly maintained the direction and coherence of the document.

Dominant characteristics

What are the salient features of the document? It is a biblical, spiritual and frequently original and perceptive meditation. An example of this is when the Pope comments on the two Pentecosts of Mary: the Annunciation for the birth of the Word Incarnate (*Luke 1: 35*), and the Pentecost which gave birth to the Church (*Acts 1: 14; 2*). In both cases, Mary's presence (discreet but essential), opens the way to the birth of the Spirit.

In the Church, too, she continues to be a maternal presence, as is shown by the words spoken from the Cross:

> 'Woman, this is your son!'
> 'This is your mother'.

The encyclical is ecumenical by virtue of this sensitive concern to use the Bible, by a return to the sources, rather than by means of diplomacy which would soften doctrine.

The encyclical is also conciliar. It endeavours to have the teaching of the Council speak for itself and thus quotes the Council more than 100 times.

The encyclical is permeated with liturgy, as we have seen, and it bears the prayerful signature of the *Alma Redemptoris Mater* which provides its opening and closing words.

The course taken by the Pope

John Paul II starts with a biblical text, the one in which Paul mentions the Mother of God, without naming her:

> When the time had fully come, God sent his Son, born of a woman ... so that we might receive adoption as sons.

The Pope points out that this text had already been the point of departure for the treatment of the Blessed Virgin Mary by the Council. This choice has ecumenical value since Luther's reform, born out of a meditation on St Paul, enlarged upon the apostle's reticence concerning the Virgin Mary. This reticence is in keeping with St Paul's own experience: knocked to the ground on the road to Damascus by the risen Christ, he remains fixated by this vision of glory and he has a certain difficulty in perceiving the Incarnation other than as a *kenosis*, or a humiliation (in contrast with the Resurrection). Unlike John, Paul does not see the 'tangible glory of the Word of life'. This is why Stephen Benko, the only Protestant who attempted to find a basic principle for establishing a 'reformed mariology', derived his principle from *Galatians 4:4*: *Mary gave Christ his kenosis, his humiliation*.

The Pope emphasises the riches of *Galatians 4:4*:

> 'Which celebrates together the love of the Father, the mission of the Son, the gift of the Spirit, the role of the woman from whom the Redeemer was born and our own divine filiation, in the mystery of the fullness of time.' (*n. 1*)

After having located in this fullness of time the coming of Christ and the dawning of the year 2000, the Pope makes a place for his dynamic theme: the pilgrimage of Mary and the Church which continues it.

The pilgrimage of faith indicates the interior history, that is, the story of souls. But it is also the story of all human beings (the Pope specifies) begun by the Virgin before Christ, in order to welcome Christ and preserve the foremost place in the people of God (n. 6).

Thus, Mary remains the Star of the Sea, the Morning Star which pierces through our night, to borrow an image from St Bernard, quoted in a footnote:

> Take away this sun which brightens our temporal world and will it still be day? Take away Mary, this star of the immense sea and what will remain, except the depth of night, the shadow of death and the thickest darkness (St Bernard, *Sermon*, op. 5).

At this point the Pope begins the three steps of his observation:

1 *Mary and Christ*

First, the relationship of the Virgin with Christ.

John Paul II approaches this by commenting on the new name, the name of grace, which Mary received from God at the Annunciation: 'Rejoice, Hail, full of grace'.

The Pope observes that the Word *charitoo*, from which is derived the new name given to Mary, *kecharitomene*, full of grace, is also the one by which the Apostle Paul signifies the grace given to all Christians. This notion is not to be translated by the French word *grâcier*, which would signify a simple pardon or reprieve, but rather by *gratifier*: object of the favour and gratuitous love of God which transfigures and transforms those whom he loves. In Mary's case, this grace is a generous gift. For her, everything has its origin in grace alone (to borrow Luther's famous adage) and for her everything is grace. She is thus the prototype of the Church and of all Christians. We have the same grace, stemming from the very love of God. There is in this an exegetical, theological and ecumenical view of great value.

After this gratuitous gift of God, the point of departure for salvation, John Paul II considers Mary's response: he stresses that it is her faith which makes her the point of departure and prototype of the Church. He gives this beautiful commentary on the initial response of Mary, her *fiat*.

> Mary entrusted herself to God completely, manifesting 'the obedience of faith ...' She responded, therefore, with all her human and feminine 'I' (par. 13).

He further states that the faith of Mary:

> first at the Annunciation and then fully at the foot of the Cross, opens an interior space within humanity which the eternal Father can fill *with every spiritual blessing*. It is the space of the 'new and eternal Covenant'. This space subsists in the Church (par. 28).

John Paul II also speaks of the *kenosis* of Mary's faith (par. 18). What does this mean? *Kenosis* is, according to St Paul, the sacrifice by which the Son of God made man 'emptied' himself in some way of his glory by the Incarnation and redemptive Passion. John Paul II demonstrates the impact of this *kenosis* on Mary's faith. At the Annunciation, he says, she heard this promise for her son:

> And now, standing at the foot of the Cross, Mary is the witness, humanly speaking, of the complete negation of these words ... Her Son hangs in agony ..., condemned, despised. How great, how heroic then is the obedience of faith shown by Mary in the face of God's 'unsearchable judgements' .... Mary is perfectly united with Christ in his *self-emptying* ...

This is perhaps the deepest *kenosis* of faith in human history (par. 18).

2 *Mary and the Church*

The second part of the encyclical considers the correlation between Mary and the Church by common reference to Christ. The title affirms 'Mother of God at the centre of the pilgrim Church', and confirms the dynamic or programmes of the encyclical.

The Church is a pilgrim. Mary began her pilgrimage at the Annunciation: 'blessed for having believed'. She illuminates the way. She remains at the centre.

The Pope recalls her presence in the upper room of Pentecost, she who had already received the Holy Spirit and is going to receive him in a new plentitude. She remains the point of departure for the apostolic Church, which participates, in a sense, in the faith of Mary (par. 27). She did not receive directly, as did the twelve (par. 26), an apostolic mission but, rather, a mission of prayer and witness as the 'unique witness of the mystery of Jesus'. (It is in this sense that Leo XIII gave her the title 'Mother of the Church', for having instructed the apostles about the infancy of Jesus which she alone knew.) In this area, she was the evangelist of the evangelists. The advance of the Church depends on faith, and Mary is its point of departure and its support.

The Pope also indicates the importance of Mary in ecumenism. He appeals especially for a strengthening of the link with the east at the hour of the millenium of holy Russia. He sees in the common devotion to the *theotokos* an aspect of unity.

He finishes by referring to the Magnificat of the pilgrim Church. He is not disturbed by the objectively revolutionary character of this canticle, which sings about a colossal reversal between the rich and the poor, the powerful and the oppressed.

In 1913, Charles Maurras, founder of *Action Française*, congratulated the Church for having stamped out 'the revolutionary venom of this canticle' to which 'Marc Sangnier and the democratic priests' appealed, way before the theologians of liberation. After having conducted an extensive dialogue with the bishops of Brazil, the Pope concluded and accepted that there was an aspect of this which was correct: a preferential option for the poor which is the programme of the gospel, and the importance of a liberation which is certainly not a political or Marxist revolution, but the one about which Mary sings: a revolution of faith, the revolution of God who does not transform yesterday's oppressed into oppressors but lays up riches for the dignity of the poor. It is in this sense that 'Mary is, at the side of her Son, the most perfect icon of freedom and of the liberation of humanity and the universe' (par. 37).

3 *Motherhood or mediation*

The third part is entitled 'Maternal mediation'. Certain people are astonished that the Pope entitled this section *mediation* and they interpret this as a blow to ecumenism. Our century began with a great deal of campaigning for the definition of Mary as 'universal Mediatrix'. But Pius XII rejected this definition and avoided the word 'Mediatrix' owing to the fact that Mary could not be said to be the Mediatrix either of graces in the Old Testament, or of sanctifying grace which is an immediate imprint of God on our souls. He also wanted to avoid obscuring the basic maxim of the Apostle Paul: Christ is *sole mediator*. The Council spoke again of Mary as Mediatrix with hesitation, against the advice of Cardinal Bea and solely to relativise the meaning of the term. Vatican II stuck to referring Mary's mediation to the unique mediation of Christ, emphasising that the 'immediate union of believers with Christ' is in no way mediated or diminished but is sustained by her. John Paul II repeats the moderate line of the Council from which he quotes extensively. He is quite insistent upon this and specifies further:

> It is 'a mediation of intercession' (this expression had been created by theologians of the seventeenth century in order to exclude a 'mediation of Redemption' which they reserved for the sole Mediator).

John Paul II repeats that this mediation is subordinate. He states that it is a mediation *in Christ*. The Protestant, Hans Asmussen, on the basis of this precision, accepted the Catholic expression. But the Pope maintains the universal character of this mediation not by making Mary the 'channel' or intermediary of each grace but because of her universal 'participation' in the unique 'Mediator'.

The Pope does not intend to provoke a return to the excesses of the pre-Conciliar period, during which the faithful expected daily homilies about Mary as Mediatrix, but forgot that Christ is the Mediator. John Paul II wished to enlarge upon the explanation of the Council by demonstrating how Mary's motherhood (like every motherhood) furnished some aspects of mediation, and how she is, in this position, concretely Mediatrix:

— At the Annunciation she consents to the plan of *God* in the name of humanity. As some Byzantine homilists put it: in this mission she is mediatrix for earth as Gabriel is for heaven.

— At Cana, she interceded with Christ for all humankind: 'They have no wine' (wine being the symbol of messianic joy), then she invites us to turn to Christ for assistance: 'Do whatever he tells you' (*John 2: 5;* par. 21).

Mary as teacher

The Pope appeals for an awareness of Mary's role in the life of the Church and of each Christian. He insists, in accordance with the Council (*Lumen gentium*, n. 63-64) on the analogy and continuity between Mary and the Church: Mary is the model of the Church on the basis of a 'relationship of exemplarity' (par. 44).

Mary also received a function as mother (par. 44). We are reminded of this maternity in 'the Eucharistic celebration, wherein Christ, his true body born of the Virgin Mary, becomes present'.

The Pope insists upon the personal character of the maternity, in the sense in which we mentioned it above: for a mother, each child is unique:

> ... the essence of motherhood is the fact that it concerns the person.

Motherhood always establishes a unique relationship between two people:

> between mother and child and between child and mother. Even when the same woman is the mother of many children, her personal relationship with each one of them is of the very essence of motherhood. For each child is generated in a unique way and this is true both for the mother and for the child.
>
> Each child is surrounded in the same way by that maternal love on which is based the child's development and coming to maturity as a human being.

This is true, the Pope continues, 'in the order of grace as in the order of nature'.

In the light of this fact it becomes easier to understand why, in Christ's testament on Golgotha, his mother's new motherhood is expressed in the singular, in reference to one man:

> 'This is your Son' (*John 19: 27,* par. 45).

In accordance with the testament and example of Christ, the Pope invites us to entrust ourselves confidently to the Virgin (which his motto, taken from Grignion de Montfort: *Totus Tuus, all for you*, expresses).

This entrusting of oneself is the response to love and, in

particular, to the love of a mother. This entrusting (in Italian, *affidamento*) is directed towards the 'consecration to Christ through the hands of Mary' (*par.* 48) since, strictly speaking, we can only consecrate ourselves to God as Grignion de Montfort taught in accordance with the masters of the French school.

John Paul II invites us to follow the example of the apostle John, in the full sense of the expression: 'He took her into his house' (*eis ta idia*), which also seems to signify: he took her 'for his own'.

In giving oneself over filially, the Christian, like the apostle John 'receives among his personal goods, the Mother of Christ and brings her into everything that makes up his inner life, that is to say, into his human and Christian 'I'. Thus the Christian seeks to be taken into that 'matured charity' with which the mother of the Redeemer 'cares for the brethren of her Son' in whose birth and development she cooperates (*Lumen gentium* n. 63; Encyclical par. 45).

The Pope comes back to this theme frequently but without explaining the role of educator which the Council attributed to Mary and which is so admirably demonstrated by the holiness of visionaries, from Catherine Labouré to Bernadette.

Yes, Mary, servant of the Lord, prepares us for the total consecration to God for which we have been stamped with the imprint of God, inscribed in the very character of baptism. Mary, our model, disposes us towards this and helps us, like a truly loving mother.

'Entrusting oneself is the response to the love of a person and in particular to the love of a mother (par. 45).' The encyclical, which speaks of the Holy Spirit (more than forty times), does not neglect to tell us that Mary's motherhood is a 'motherhood' in the spirit (par. 44) and in the 'communion of the saints' (par. 41). This is the same thing, since the Holy Spirit stirred and enflamed first Mary, then the Church, communion of saints in Jesus Christ, to which he extends the initial communion of faith and body between Christ and his Mother.

By way of conclusion, the Pope insists upon the connection between the millennium of Holy Russia and the preparation for the second millennium so that the people 'fallen down be lifted up' (as the formula of the *Alma Redemptoris Mater* runs: *Succurre cadenti surgere qui curat populo*).

Presence of Mary (par. 47)
The Holy Father indicates: 'I would like to stress the special presence of the Mother of God'. He has by now mentioned it more than ten times (pars. 3, 5, 51, 53, 54, 61, 62, 81, 84, 101, 102; cf 17 and 71). His encyclical is therefore an invitation to rediscover the presence of Mary. I was not familiar with the encyclical when I wrote this book as an invitation to rediscover her presence (cf. sub-title in Chapter 4). This idea came to me not only from Christian tradition and from the position of the Church which has too often forgotten this presence, but from Grignion de Montfort, who inspired the Pope, and from my involvement, over many years, with de Montfort's teaching on the Virgin. Let us rediscover the living presence of Mary our mother: supreme gift of Jesus Christ on Calvary, before his final breath was succeeded by the new breath of the Resurrection. This double sign gives to the disciples the Holy Spirit which Mary had been the first to receive. Mary is inseparable from the Spirit who sustains her (*Luke 1:35*).

APPENDIX III

Salient points of the encyclical

The beginning
The mother of the Redeemer has a precise place in the plan of salvation, for 'when the time had fully come, God sent forth his Son, born of woman, born under the law, to redeem those who were under the law so that we might receive adoption as sons. And because you are sons, God has sent the Spirit of his Son into our hearts, crying 'Abba! Father!' ' (*Galatians 4:4-6*).

With these words of the apostle Paul, which the Second Vatican Council takes up at the beginning of its treatment of the Blessed Virgin Mary, I too wish to begin my reflection on the role of Mary *in the mystery of Christ* and on *her active and exemplary presence in the life of the Church*. For they are words which celebrate together the *love of the Father*, the mission of the Son, the gift of the Spirit, the role of the woman from whom the Redemer was born and our own divine filiation, in the mystery of the 'fullness of time'. (Par. 1)

Kenosis of faith for Mary on Golgotha

At that moment she had also heard the words: 'He will be great... and the Lord God will give to him the throne of his father David, and he will reign over the house of Jacob forever; and of his Kingdom there will be no end' (*Luke 1:32-33*).

And now, standing at the foot of the cross, Mary is the witness, humanly speaking, *of the complete negation of these words*. On that wood of the cross her son hangs in agony as one condemned. 'He was despised and rejected by men; a man of sorrows... he was despised, and we esteemed him not': as one destroyed (cf. *Isaiah 53:3-5*). How great, how heroic then is the *obedience* of faith shown by Mary in the face of God's 'unsearchable judgments'! How completely she 'abandons herself to God' without reserve, 'offering the full assent of the intellect and the will' to him whose 'ways are inscrutable' (cf *Romans 11:33*)! And how powerful too is the action of grace in her soul, how all-pervading is the influence of the Holy Spirit and of his light and power!

Through this faith Mary is perfectly united with Christ in his self-emptying. For 'Christ Jesus, who, though he was in the form of God, did not count equality with God a thing to be grasped, but emptied himself, taking the form of a servant, being born in the likeness of men': Precisely on Golgotha 'he humbled himself and became obedient unto death, even death on a cross' (cf. *Philippians 2:5-8*). At the foot of the cross Mary shares through faith in the shocking mystery of this self-emptying. This is perhaps the deepest *kenosis* of faith in human history. (Par. 18)

Kenosis is, according to the apostle Paul, the sacrifice by which Christ, having become man, 'emptied' himself in some way of his glory through the Incarnation and his redemptive death. John Paul II sees a reflection of this *kenosis* in the faith of Mary.

Mary and interior space

One could perhaps speak of a specific 'geography' of faith and Marian devotion which includes all these special places of pilgrimage where the people of God seek to meet the mother of God in order to find, within the radius of the maternal presence of her 'who believed', a strengthening of their own faith. For in Mary's faith, first at the annunciation and then fully at the foot of the cross, an interior space was reopened within humanity which the eternal Father can fill 'with every spiritual blessing'. It is the space 'of the new and eternal covenant', and it continues to exist in the Church, which in Christ is 'a kind of sacrament or sign of intimate union with God and of the unity of all mankind'. (Par. 28)

Mary and the Eucharist

Her motherhood is particularly noted and experienced by the Christian people at the Sacred Banquet — the liturgical celebration of the mystery of the redemption — at which Christ, his true body born of the Virgin Mary, becomes present. (Par. 44)

For a mother each child is special

Of the essence of motherhood is the fact that it concerns the person. Motherhood always establishes a unique and unrepeatable relationship between two people: between mother and child and between child and mother. Even when the same woman is the mother of many children, her personal relationship with each one of them is of the very essence of motherhood. For each child is generated in a unique and unrepeatable way, and this is true both for the mother and for the child. Each child is surrounded in the same way by that maternal love on which are based the child's development and coming to maturity as a human being.

It can be said that motherhood 'in the order of grace' preserves the analogy with what 'in the order of nature' characterises the union between mother and child. In the light of this fact it becomes easier to understand why in Christ's testament on Golgotha his mother's new motherhood is expressed in the singular, in reference to one man: 'Behold your son'. (Par. 45)

Mary and feminism

This Marian dimension of Christian life takes on special importance in relation to women and their status. In fact, femininity has a unique relationship with the mother of the Redeemer, a subject which can be studied in greater depth elsewhere. Here I simply wish to note that the figure of Mary of Nazareth sheds light on womanhood as such by the very fact that God, in the sublime event of the incarnation of his Son, entrusted himself to the ministry, the free and active ministry of a woman. It can thus be said that women, by looking to Mary, find in her the secret of living their femininity with dignity and of achieving their own true advancement.

Ecumenism and the millennium in Russia

It is also appropriate to mention the icon of Our Lady of Vladimir, which continually accompanied the pilgrimage of faith of the people of ancient Rus. The first millennium of the conversion of those noble lands to Christianity is approaching: lands of humble folk, of thinkers and of saints. The icons are still venerated in the Ukraine, in Byelorussia and in Russia under various titles. They are the images which witness to the faith and spirit of prayer of that people, who sense the presence and protection of the mother of God.

Such a wealth of praise, built up by the different forms of the Church's great tradition, could help us to hasten the day when the Church can begin once more to breathe fully with her 'two lungs', the East and the West. As I have often said, this is more than ever necessary today. It would be an effective aid in furthering the progress of the dialogue already taking place between the Catholic Church and the Churches and ecclesial communities of the West. It would also be the way for the pilgrim Church to sing and to live more perfectly her Magnificat.

As has already been mentioned, many among our divided brethren also honour and celebrate the mother of the Lord, especially Eastern Christians. It is a marian light cast upon ecumenism. In particular, I wish to mention once more that during the marian year there will occur the millennium of the baptism of St Vladimir, grand duke of Kiev (988). This marked the beginning of Christianity in the territories of what was then called Rus, and subsequently in other territories of Eastern Europe. In this way, through the work of evangelisation Christianity spread beyond Europe, as far as the northern territories of the Asian continent. We would therefore like especially during this year to join in prayer with all those who are celebrating the millenium of this baptism, both Orthodox and Catholics. (Pars. 33, 34, and 50)